Kari and Noelle have survived with honor and balance; now they have the credentials to help others. *When He Leaves* will give uplifting and inspirational challenges to the women who have endured overwhelming loss from a broken marriage. It will jump-start them on the road to becoming well again and prove to be a handbook for women who feel they cannot make a fresh start.

     ~ Barbara Johnson, author
Stick a Geranium in Your Hat and Be Happy

As a professor of clinical psychology and a therapist, I greatly look forward to recommending this work to my students, clients, and all who suffer similarly—as well as to professionals in helping positions. Displaying the vivid colors of dyes extracted from intense emotions, this volume offers hope, encouragement, and direction.

     ~ Gary H. Strauss, Ed.D., assistant professor
Rosemead School of Psychology, Biola University

A fabulous work of hope and direction for any woman who has loved and lost. The authors share how the plot of our lives is never as we expect, yet there is One who never leaves. The answers are here, written with a lyrical quality, embroidered with honesty, and woven with the eternal truths of Scripture.

     ~ Robin Jones Gunn, author
best-selling Christian romance novelist

With powerful scab-scraping honesty, empathy, vulnerability, what encouragement and hope-giving is contained in these pages. I'm a woman living out the truth of this book, learning and growing by every wonderful sentence. The emotions, thoughts, the soul of it are exactly where I have been—and am. I want to cut out so many thoughts and paste them all over my home, but then my book would look like my heart used to look.

     ~ Dr. Karen J. Hayter, host and producer
COPE, nationwide call-in television program

This book is important for pastors and those working with the divorced. They must see the extreme trauma and sense of alienation from Christian fellowship that can often accompany this tragedy. As portrayed and supported in this book, the proclamation of grace and forgiveness in divorce does not dilute Christian standards. It rather strengthens them.

~ Paul E. Larsen, president
The Evangelical Covenant Church

An empowering book for women experiencing the crucible of divorce. Writing with unique perspectives, Kari and Noelle do not sugarcoat the pain and consequences, but offer hope that God can rebuild the broken places. I believe this book will be a cherished how-to-survive manual for those who want to go from being a victim to one who triumphs.

~ Nancie Carmichael, editor at large
Virtue

Rooted in vivid, realistic experience, this book deserves to rise to the top of the lists for women in whatever stage of divorce. Written with luminous descriptive and analytical skills, sayings and sidebars will be copied and kept on refrigerator doors. I applaud this fine work.

~ Dwight Small, professor emeritus, Westmont College,
author, *Remarriage and God's Redeeming Grace*

I liked this book for its examples. Kari and Noelle shared their lives and gave us a view. They stood with their pain. Through acceptance and persistence, they found what every redeemed, divorced woman discovers "when he leaves." God's grace is sufficient.

~ Ingrid Trobisch, author, speaker,
founder, Family Life Mission

If he leaves, he leaves. But the broken pieces of your life don't have to stay. No matter what you've thought, prayed, said, or heard since your divorce, you haven't heard enough until you've read West and Quinn. Usher them in to share how to convert anger into forgiveness, disgust into direction, and shame into celebration. Just when you thought you couldn't face tomorrow, here's hope for every woman abandoned by her mate, every counselor's resource shelf, and every friend wanting to listen more effectively.

〜 Phyllis Wallace, host
Woman To Woman, Lutheran Hour Ministries

Finally someone wrote the book that was screaming to be written! In a topic often swept under the carpet and awkwardly dealt with, the wound is finally getting some attention. A surprise: I discovered a treasure trove of principles to guide me through totally unrelated hurts, tragedies, confusion of my own.

〜 Bruce Marchiano, actor who portrayed Jesus,
Video Bible production of *The Gospel of Matthew*

Unexpected in its candor. Stirring in the courage to write what is unspeakably private. Important in its insistence on confronting betrayal. All with an insistent belief in God's grace. I know these authors, have seen them cry, and watched their struggle to believe again. The corporate experience of two women defies trite answers. This is a story for everyone who has believed in the power of love.

〜 Jeanette Thomason, editor
Aspire

When He Leaves

Choosing to
Live,
Love, and
Laugh Again

When He Leaves

Kari West & Noelle Quinn

Chariot VICTOR
PUBLISHING
A DIVISION OF COOK COMMUNICATIONS

Victor Books is an imprint of
Cook Communications, Colorado Springs, Colorado 80918
Cook Communications, Paris, Ontario
Kingsway Communications, Eastbourne, England

Editor: Lorraine M. Davis
Cover Design/Art Direction: Bill Gray
Interior: Big Cat Studios

2 3 4 5 6 7 8 9 10 Printing/Year 02 01 00

Library of Congress Cataloging-in-Publication Data

West, Kari.
      When he leaves: choosing to live, love, and laugh again/by Kari West and
Noelle Quinn.
            p. cm.
      Includes bibliographical references.
      ISBN 1-56476-699-3
      1. Divorced women—Psychology. 2. Divorced women—Religious life.
3. Divorce—Psychological aspects. 4. Divorce—Religious aspects—Christianity.
5. Separation (Psychology) I. Quinn, Noelle. II. Title.
HQ814.W48 1998
306.89'082—dc21   97-31722
                                                                                   CIP

Dedicated to Women

Those who played a part in our lives,
the few whose selfless efforts made this book possible
and the many who, reading these words,
know exactly why we wrote them.

∽ Acknowledgments

We are indebted to all those who believed we could talk about divorce with redemption. Humiliation with dignity. Private pain with transparency and truth.

Julie Smith and Lorraine Davis, our caring, keen-eyed editors, for understanding the message for women we wanted to convey.

Arlene Somerville and Jeanette Thomason for reading the finished manuscript on midnight oil after working day jobs. Dwight Small, Steve Severs, and The Hayward Area Christian Writers Group for their feedback. Patricia Cousins and the reference librarians at the Alameda County Library for collateral information.

Sharon Kinard, interceding for our protection throughout the writing process. Ethel Herr and the Literature Ministry Prayer Fellowship who faithfully prayed for our discernment. Ingrid Trobisch and Pastor Larry Vold for their inspiration.

Our parents for loving us and raising us to love our husbands and families.

Kari's husband, Richard, for his support, encouragement, and affirmation.

Our gratitude to Mt. Hermon Christian Writers Conference, Mt. Hermon, California, for bringing us together.

And to God who gave us grace.

∿ Table of Contents

~ Foreword

*W*ithin every life story, there is a love story—first love, rekindled love, or love lost. Like moths, we are drawn to love's flame here in this book. Flipping through scribbled journals, we will ourselves to come close to the pain. Not being consumed by it as we hold it in hand is the miracle of what we know.

No silence is loud enough to drown the echoes of our experience; that is why we write. But our words shed only a flicker of light on a much larger picture. This is a composite of two separate sets of circumstances as well as the meeting of two unique stories. There is much more we do not say than we do. We juggle the enormity of what we felt needed to be said with saying nothing at all. We cannot give you the definitive account. We give you our personal reflections on truth that surfaced as we searched for our voice and footing in this most earthy of human errors, divorce.

Our joint desire is not to air dirty laundry, dump our garbage in your backyard, or get even with our ex-spouses, both brilliant men whom we wish well. Their names and those of our families and others have been changed. We write not to be provocative or sensational, and we intend no malice. We are not bitter, although we are frustrated by the trend of wives dumped in midlife, children abandoned, and the response of the church to a crisis that occurs no less frequently within evangelicalism than outside it.

Although we fought to keep our marriages intact until the very end, we have since gone on with our lives. In the course of that, we hear the screams of women. That is our bottom line. For the many who journey this way, the many who will travel the same path, as well as those who want to understand, we write. But this is not just an appeal to the intelligence and emotions of women.

We hope every church leader and worker—especially those involved in men's and women's ministries—will read this account and wrestle through these issues with us for the sake of other families.

Between the two of us we have four daughters, quite an investment in femininity. Innocent and accomplished, they mean more to us than words can say. They may choose never to read our stories, but our daily prayer is that they find healing and one day be cherished by mates who are faithful and true. Our desire is that each enjoy a healthy ongoing relationship with her father.

To frightened souls looking for courage to take steps back into life, love, and laughter, opening the pages of this book may mean that you, too, will touch your pain. We understand; read it at random, a quote now and then, or a chapter out of order. Absorb what you can, when you can. Then write to us.

We have been through something profound. This book is our labor of love.

∼ Introduction

You are not alone. You belong to a sacred sisterhood, the wounded, the rejected, the betrayed. You are seeing truth and in the horror of its light, are shaken, battered, and bruised. But you do not give up. You get onto bloodied knees and start to crawl forward again. Like a drowning woman, you reach out for a life-saver, anything floating.

You are not thinking about recovery or rebuilding or happiness right now. You just want to survive. For your kids. For your parents. For some unexplained something deep down inside that makes you hang on even when you'd rather slide into the cold waters, be submerged, and disappear.

It would be better to die, you sometimes tell yourself. But something keeps you coming up for air, more light, more truth. You pray for the courage to stand what you see. A week, a month, a year seem too long to count. You hope for the strength to get through the next moment, the next hour, the next day.

We have come through these same waters. Deep waters. We know the feelings, the fears, the rage, the terror. Let us take your hand, put an arm around your shoulder, swim beside you for a while. We cannot bring you to safety. Only you can find the life-ring that will finally pull you up and out of the cold and the dark. But we can whisper, *Hang on! Hold out!*

By the goodness of God our Father, the same God you may have cursed a time or two, you will find the way. In the comfort of the Holy Spirit who is closer than your breath, you will know increasing degrees of peace, sanity, and at last—at long last—joy. In the fellowship of the Son, Jesus Christ, you are loved and accepted exactly as you are, desired, and enfolded in arms tender and strong.

You are graceful, beautiful, and sensual. You are to be treasured and cherished. Proverbs 4:18 says you are like the light of dawn, growing brighter and brighter until full daylight. We wait with you and watch. You'll see.

∼ Kari and Noelle

1

We Know You

I am afraid.
My courage is gone.
I lift my hands to you in prayer.
As a dry land needs rain, I thirst for you.
Lord, answer me quickly.
I am getting weak.

~ Psalm 143:4,6-7, NCV

We would know you anywhere. We see you everywhere: crossing a street, sitting behind stacks of paperwork at the next desk in the office, waiting in line at the grocery checkout, serving as greeter at the church door on Sunday morning. We see you at the gym, the PTA, the Bible study potluck, the county fair and the doctor's office. Sometimes we ask, "How are you?" and you always answer, "Fine!" or "Great!" but we know the truth.

We notice what many others do not: the limp smile disguising your fear, the lump in your throat right above your gold necklace, the pain deep in your eyes that no makeup can cover. Sometimes, if we venture closer, we feel the ground quivering beneath your feet. We sense the path you're on and sigh about what lies before you.

We've felt the jabbing pain you feel when you hear the love song you shared with him, when you hear two lovers say, "I love you." You think no one will whisper those words in your ear again.

And that family picture in the church directory? "Okay, now," the photographer said, "everybody think love." No one knew you were thinking daisies.... *He loves me not.*

We know about the photo albums in your cupboard and the way you avoid that corner of your house. We know about that treasured recipe book you tossed out in fury, the one full of favorite requests you cooked for him through years of mealtimes. You have his love letters tied with ribbon in your bedroom closet.

21

Your engagement ring and wedding band lie in the bottom of your dresser drawer, and you wonder what to do with them. Your eyes fill with tears at odd moments during your working day and you hope no one notices.

At night, you've tried to put odd shapes and sizes of ragged suspicions together. You tried confronting him, but he always talked you out of it. *Love believes the best.* Doesn't the Bible say that? *Love never gives up.*

But his working late became more and more frequent. Sometimes he left for work early or refused to get out of bed until you and the children had left for the day. He'd crawl in late, and he didn't want to see anyone the next morning. He fussed about the noise the children made. And how dare you inquire about where he was—working for you, of course; earning a living, of course. Or sometimes he just said, "Give me space. Get off my case. You have nothing to worry about."

Once he told you his office phone was out of order and you'd have to leave a message if you needed to get hold of him. You never suspected he wasn't there at all. Another time, he left a party early to go back to work, just after your friend and neighbor excused herself to go home. You never thought a dishonorable thought about them.

When you said, "Let's make love tonight," he'd say, "I'm tired," or "I don't feel good." He obliged when you initiated, but his responses became less passionate. When you asked, "What's wrong?" he shrugged it off: "Oh, lots of men my age are impotent," or "I'm fine. I just don't feel like it tonight." You would lie in the darkness and pray he'd touch you back. But his touch became more and more infrequent even during the day. Your insecurities mounted, distancing him even more.

Love in action is a harsh and dreadful thing,
compared with love in dreams.

∿ Fyodor Mikhaylovich Dostoyevsky

When you finally found the nerve to ask the right questions of yourself and of him, he accused you: "You just don't get it." "You're too sensitive." "You're too black-and-white."

During a fight, he may have snarled, "You're crazy," or "What man would ever want you?" When you pleaded for romance and intimacy, he may have quipped, "Our marriage is fine. We'll do the best we can with what we have. It'll get better." And you believed him—until the roof started caving in on top of you.

Maybe a friend risked saying, "Do you think he's having an affair?" You probably answered, "No. Not him. He'd never do that. We're a Christian family. We pray together, attend church." Maybe he is the one who raised his hands in praise, led the worship, helped with the young people's program. Perhaps he's the choir director, the youth leader, the elder, the deacon, the Bible-study leader—maybe even the pastor.

Another friend ventured, "Are you meeting his sexual needs?" Only you know the doubts you've agonized over, the magazine articles you've pored over, the questions you've put to your doctor, feeling desperate and determined.

Now, he is gone.

You are devastated by the images of what you did not know, you did not recognize, you could not admit. The accumulated pieces start to fall into place. Each unrelated message bouncing through your brain is beginning to make sense.

> *When I can't express what I really feel,*
> *I practice feeling what I can express and none of it*
> *is equal I know; but that's why mankind alone*
> *among the mammals learns to cry.*

> ∾ Nikki Giovanni

We feel your searing humiliation and staggering pain. We hear your rage at yourself, at him, and at God. You ask, "How could this happen to me?" You wonder, *Does anybody care?*

We do. We are just like you.

We know the pathway you've been on, every stone you've stumbled over, the muddy ruts, the crevices leading off the edge.

We understand how you've thought so many times, *Something is wrong with this picture.* You kept telling yourself, *I cannot dwell on this.* You went on, distracted by the many duties and responsibilities before you. And that is just what he wanted.

Even as the confusion and hurt accumulated, you kept making meals, cleaning house, and caring for the children of a man who had long since left you in his heart and mind. So many people were counting on you: children, parents, friends, the church. Months passed. Years. Then one day the pot overflowed, the lies reached their zenith, the deceit could no longer be hidden.

You inhaled deception and exhaled horror. Now you wonder how you'll ever get yourself to your OB/GYN and ask for a set of STD and HIV tests. How to explain the pain of your humiliation or the indirect way he threatened your life. You tell a counselor, "I can't be divorced. I can't be a single mom. I can't *do this.* This isn't how I planned my life."

You wonder how to tell your children. You promised they would never live in a "broken family," that you and their daddy would never get a divorce. How do you comfort them now or quell their fears when you have so many of your own?

We know. We, too, have stretched across an empty bed and howled into the black arms of the night. We are here to talk about those sacred, private spaces and the healing on its way to you.

2

Kari's
Snapshots

I am seven years old. My mother lifts the lid on the cedar trunk at the foot of her bed, takes out a red fox boa, and drapes it around my shoulders. I squeal with delight, feeling glamorous and beautiful. I twirl like a top, my mind dancing in a world of Prince Charming's kisses and his forever love.

...Mother sings a hymn to me: "I would be *true*, for there are those who trust me. I would be *pure*, for there are those who care. I would be *strong*, for there is much to suffer. I would be *brave*, for there is much to dare."[1] Each night I fall asleep to music on my radio. A Christian program leads me to Jesus.

Memory is a diary that we carry around with us.

~ Oscar Wilde

..."Start praying for your future husband," the Sunday School teacher tells our ninth-grade girls' class. "Don't look for the right person; be the right person."
. . . At eighteen, I perch alone on a twin bed in sparse surroundings. Home is a rented room on the eleventh floor of a boarding-house two thousand miles from my parents. I work days to pay for room, board, and night-school tuition. Listening to the grinding growl of buses on the street below, I'm content and happy, reading a love letter. Ed is stationed back east in the military. I met

him at my home church last Christmas. Snow fell as he kissed me good-bye.

> *Love has various lodgings;*
> *The same word does not always signify*
> *the same thing.*
>
> ∼ Voltaire

…I'm twenty-two, in a bouffant wedding dress, walking down an aisle in shimmering candlelight. Ed promises, "Until death do us part." The minister prays, "May the Holy Spirit lead you into all truth." I smile and treasure Ed's words. Years later it is the minister's words I'll remember.

…Through the years, my job supports us while Ed completes his undergraduate and graduate degrees. I dream of being a stay-at-home mom.

…Thirteen years later, I overhear a young woman at work tell another, "I want my marriage to be just like Ed and Kari's." Hopping into the elevator, I'm proud and happy. We have a two-story house with a water view and a darling three-year-old daughter, Melanie.

…Ed buys himself a flashy sports car. When Melanie and I visit my parents for a week in the midwest, he purchases a motorcycle. Home again, I voice concern about little Melanie going for a ride. He accuses me of not trusting him, straps her to his belt, and guns the bike down the street. I think, *Wherever Ed is heading, I'm in his way.*

> *Mockery is the weapon that evil uses powerfully*
> *to strip its victim of a sense of self and life.*
>
> ∼ Dr. Dan Allender

...I injure my back. Ed complains when I ask his help making our bed, so I do it alone, crawling around its edges on my knees. Later, one Sunday afternoon, I walk into the family room. He is stretched out in his favorite chair. A porn video flickers on the TV screen. "What are you doing?" I ask. "Our four year old is upstairs; what if she walks in here?"

"You're always starting fights," Ed says.

...Melanie's first-grade teacher recommends testing for behavioral and school problems. After Melanie is diagnosed with hyperactivity and a learning disability, I research the Feingold diet in my "spare" time. I'm hesitant about subjecting her to drug therapy and decide instead to cook meals free of artificial flavorings, colors, and preservatives. It takes hours to check packaging labels at the market, to bake cakes so Melanie can bring a piece to eat at another child's birthday party, to attend parents' support-group meetings, and to tutor her after dinner. Ed doesn't believe the diagnosis and says we can't afford for me to quit work. *Doesn't anybody understand I'm not sure how much more I can handle?*

...Melanie is taping her daddy's latest note to the railing of her canopy bed. Ed places one on her pillow each time he leaves on a business trip, a "so-called" group-counseling retreat, or weekend getaway. He says he's fighting memories of his mother's abandonment and his parents' divorce. I try to understand and give him the space and time he needs to heal. I read every book in the library and Christian bookstore on midlife crisis and childhood trauma. But the answers don't connect with my questions. I think about all the notes above Melanie's bed. They bother me. But there is no one to ask about it. Someone did tell me Ed has a spiritual problem. It was close to the truth, but knowing it doesn't help.

...When I can fit it in, I exercise twice a week. At the gym, I find a note tucked beneath my car's wiper blades: "Your husband is fooling around in your own backyard."

Ed claims somebody at work is just playing political games. He plans to take it to the sheriff's office to have the handwriting checked. Grabbing the note, he says, "But I know you—you'll make a big deal out of this."

...Warm water winds its way through the strands of my hair, bouncing off my shoulders, trickling down my back, spilling onto the tiles. I turn my face into the spray, praying for truth. My daughter can't hear me heave and sob when I'm here. Soap is a good excuse for puffy, red eyes. I come here more often now—whenever Ed's excuses and accusations pummel my mind like bricks.

It is only with the heart that one can see rightly; what is essential is invisible to the eye.

⌇ Antoine de Saint-Exupéry

...The minister who counsels us keeps telling me I'm the stronger one and Ed is going through a midlife crisis. So for Melanie and me, I recommit myself to my man and my marriage once again. But now I'm pleading for truth.

...I round the hill known as age forty and feel less sure of my life. Ed and I are back together after a seven-month separation so he could "find himself." I work extra hours to provide a down payment for a weekend cabin in the moutains to give us a second chance, a new dream. Driving up to the cabin one weekend, he asks me to adjust the mirror on the passenger side. I tug and pull and then sigh, "It won't budge."

"Hurry, Mommy, I'm cold," Melanie says.

"You're so stupid!" Ed mutters. "Can't you do anything right?"

"Yeah, Mom, can't you do anything right?" Melanie wraps her arms around her daddy's neck and snuggles in.

What did I do wrong? I wonder.

...Ed's away again for the weekend. It's dark by the time I slide onto the organ bench in the living room, caressing the keys with my fingers. "Because He lives, I can face tomorrow." I can barely see the notes and words through my tears. Something is wrong. I can't sort my scattered thoughts.

A faintly penciled note Melanie left on the kitchen counter haunts me: "Dear Mom and Dad, I'm getting tired of you guys fighting and I always have to go to my room. I feel like I'm not part of this family. This house is always full of cries and hurt hearts."

I hold her up to God as I play the next verse, "This child can face uncertain days because He lives." How often have I imagined reaching for the doorknob? But I can't yank Melanie out of the only life she knows. Just because I'm hurting, I can't hurt her. My hands tremble as I play the last verse: "And then some day I'll fight life's final war with pain."[2]

Next time I will forget about love and fall into chocolate.

∽ Kari

...Ed refuses to attend church now—or fix the washing machine. He never holds my hand anymore or wants sex. He says if it's so important I should get my calendar out and schedule it, so he can service me. I cry. He calls me "too sensitive." "Crazy." I retreat emotionally.

...Ed works later and rises earlier, saying, if I inquire, that he's not accountable to me.

"But I'm your wife," I say. His dark eyes scare me.

..."Look at yourself! You're a nervous wreck," says my friend Regina. "I've never seen you like this. I know you don't believe in divorce, but are you honoring God with your marriage?"

…One weekend, Melanie, now twelve, blurts out: "You don't even know where your own husband is."

I'm suspended in disbelief.

When I looked for good, evil came to me;
And when I waited for light, then came darkness.
My heart is in turmoil and cannot rest.

       ~ Job 30:26-27

…"Ed, we need to talk," I get the courage to say again. "Can't we do something?"

He slams his body against the back of his recliner as he flings the TV remote across the room. "And just what do you suggest this time?" he counters.

"Anything! Counseling again? Another separation? I don't know! Divorce?" I say in desperation, trying to shake his usual mode of shutting me out.

"That's it! Divorce!" Ed cuts me off midsentence as if he's in a hurry. As if he's been waiting for me to say that word.

…Fourteen days before Christmas, I sort the mail, a stack of season's greetings in one hand, a divorce summons in the other. That moment slashes twenty-two years of family holiday traditions and memories. I think back to cozy evenings before the fire, listening to carols and reminiscing over photos of a growing daughter sitting on Santa's knee.

Then I remember yesterday. Melanie screamed at me: "I don't want to be anything like you. I don't want to talk like you, dress like you, act like you, or look like you because Daddy left you!"

I always trusted in a God who could turn evil into good. I wonder how He'll do it this time.

…I believe God will reward my faithfulness with a miracle before the divorce is final. I kneel beside the bed and pray, *Lord, I can't take much more.*

He whispers, "Let go and I will bless you." But I think I'm hearing things. *Letting go isn't what I want. I love Ed. I love being married. There are no grounds for this divorce.*

There is a time for departure
even when there is no certain place to go.

~ Tennessee Williams

... "I've never been happier," Ed tells me, carrying the final box to his car. He says we should have divorced a long time ago.

"What?" I ask. "You can't mean that!"

Ed stammers. "I mean . . . earlier, so we don't have to hurt Melanie," he says with a cocky toss of the head.

"Is there another woman?"

"No. But you have your desertion. And by the time the divorce is final, you'll have your infidelity," he says. "I like bleached blondes with lots of makeup and long painted nails." He gets in the car and drives off.

I stare at my short fingernails. *All those years I worked for us?* In a place beyond tears, I sob.

..."I'm glad you found out about the neighbor," says an acquaintance I haven't seen in ten years. She stands ahead of me in line at the bank the day after Ed and I finalize the paperwork and divide our assets.

"What neighbor?" I ask.

My friend shakes her head, then hurries toward the next available teller's window.

Oh, that I had wings like a dove!
For then I would fly away and be at rest.
. . . I would hasten my escape
From the windy storm and tempest.

~ Psalm 55:6, 8

…Moving the car out of the garage one morning, my eye targets a stack of Playboy magazines under some junk Ed left behind. I also find a book about how to tell when people are lying. I wonder, *What else don't I know?*

…Melanie dials Ed's residence before school. A woman answers. Melanie dials again, convinced she has the wrong number. The female voice answers again.

"Just the cleaning lady," her dad later explains when she reaches him at the office.

I drive Melanie to school. "Mom, cleaning ladies don't answer telephones," she says.

I need to deal with this, but my job for the day is already assigned. Before getting on the freeway, I race back to the house and call Ed. "Even Melanie knows what you're up to," I say.

"You made sure of that, didn't you?" he says.

No, Ed, I never knew until now, I say to myself as I place the receiver in its cradle. *I've always believed you—until now.*

…I move into the darkest tunnel of my life. I can't concentrate on my job. At night I toss and turn with dark, angry thoughts. It seems as if every day I learn something new about Ed: his secret post-office box, the names of "friends" he had traveled with, that he'd given "her" a necklace identical to one he'd given me, that "group counseling" and "bowling" were two of many cover-ups. I flip through my Bible searching for answers, scribbling each promise I find in its margins and in a journal. With trembling hands I write angry letters to God, full of fear and disappointment. Somehow I must will myself to believe He still has plans for me. *Lord,* I pray, *give me courage for each day.*

…I sit across from Ed at a restaurant, signing our last joint tax return. He looks straight at me and says, "After what I did to you, you'll never trust anyone again."

My scalp lifts. I shiver before glancing past him, over his shoulder to the view outside. An ocean breeze tugs the tucked sails on the boats nestled at the harbor. A seagull soars above steel-gray water. I reach for the pen and know I've chosen the only path, the way out, the way beyond.

> **Laugh and the world laughs with you.**
> **Cry and the world's TV networks want to make**
> **a mini-series based on your tragedy.**
>
> ∿ Shoebox Greetings
> (©1996, distributed by Universal Press Syndicate)

...Moving on and into my own house is scary. My car breaks down. The sink leaks. The stove thermostat malfunctions. Melanie walks blocks to catch the city bus to and from school. Behavior problems escalate as her grades plummet.

I tiptoe into her bedroom. Gifts from Ed fill shelves—TV, stereo system, bowling ball, stuffed animals, leather jacket, fifty-dollar perfume, a dozen roses. Standing above Melanie's sleeping form, I whisper, "Protect her, Lord. Help me release her to You."

...One weekend, when Ed picks up Melanie, he tells me he isn't sure he has ever told anybody the truth; that the worst lies are the ones he tells himself.

"And I loved you," I reply.

"I know," he says. "I wish you didn't. It would make it easier."

Wedged between compassion, numbness, and rage, I decide I am finally through reasoning with Ed. I don't want to hear another lie. I am tired of obsessing about whom he is with, where he is, and what they are doing. I tell his dad on the phone, "I hope Ed dies of AIDS." Then I ask God to forgive me and help me determine to forgive Ed—not just for what he did but for what might be ahead. *Lord, I'm trusting you for my health, Melanie, my job, car, and the unknown future,* I pray.

Me, a single-again working mom, with time for a future?

Impossible. My most blissful dream is falling asleep and never waking up.

…Today, ten years later, I don't want to remember the pain of that nightmare before Christmas—or the horror after. But I force myself to think about Ed's icy glares, his fists hitting the kitchen counter, the way he blamed me for ruining his life, how I cringed whenever his car pulled into the garage.

Ed seemed unendingly brash and insensitive. "To celebrate our amicable divorce," he said once, "I'll take you to dinner."

Celebrate? I thought. *You've left family, you're sleeping with someone else, and the ink isn't even dry on our settlement agreement.*

But I chuckle now. My future was God's surprise. I found a job closer to home, got another car, and happily gained back the weight I'd lost. I fell in love again. Richard says I'm his best friend.

And Melanie? A while back she asked, "Mom, can I wear one of your necklaces tonight?"

I smiled, remembering the days when she didn't want to talk, dress, act, or look like me.

The failure of my first marriage to Ed was not a finish, but a fresh start. I realize I am writing for all of us—you, the reader; my daughter; and myself. I believe this book will give Melanie no imformation she does not already have. Should she choose to read these words, I cherish the belief she will gain understanding of the refining process I went through and the person I am becoming. I found out when you can't go back, you go forward. I bought new photo albums, and I am just beginning to fill them. Now that's cause for celebration!

God is here this moment in the darkroom of your life.
Let Him develop the negatives into a positive image
of His character to make you more like Jesus
and to give you a future and a hope.

        ∼ Kari

3

Noelle's Snapshots

I am walking down the sidewalk in the frilly blue-and-white ballet dress my mother sewed, pink slippers tucked under my arm. The studio is at the end of the block. At five years old, I feel independent and proud of myself. I am learning just how wonderful I am. When I grow up, I am going to dance stories on a beautiful stage.

...My first day of kindergarten I see something I'd only dreamed of: a dollhouse filled with accessories. I kneel down and start to play with it, putting baby in the cradle, moving mother to the kitchen, seating father in the armchair. I imagine my someday-self in my someday-home. But I feel intimidated when another child comes along and moves things around. *Why is she taking it away from me?* I turn away, crying.

**The Lord is close to the brokenhearted
and saves those who are crushed in spirit.**

~ Psalm 34:18, NIV

...It's dark, but the bonfire is glowing on the last night of junior-high church camp. Our speaker, a missionary to the Philippines, asks us to throw a piece of wood in the fire and make our commitment to God. I sense His call to be a missionary. As I throw my piece of wood into the flames, I silently say yes to God and mean it with all my heart.

39

...*Cow bells clink in the distance. I can't believe I'm in Switzerland!* There'll be porridge and hot milk before we start our day working in the chalet or studying. Midway through college, I'm meeting young people from all over during a summer in Europe. The Christians here seem more spiritually alive than the Americans at my Christian college at home. I love Europe. I promise myself I'll be back.

...Four years later, I marry Dan under an oak tree in California. He carves our initials in its bark. I carry a bouquet of tiny roses, standing barefoot in the grass. He sings Noel Paul Stookey's "Wedding Song" to me: "The union of your spirits here is now and to remain. For whenever two or more of you are gathered in His name, there is love."[1]

My dreams of going back to Europe are coming true. We are heading there to evangelize. Dan is the man I prayed for, a man who loves God with a single heart.

We settle into our first home, two rooms in an old-world city church. Dan moves in borrowed furniture. I decorate with remnants of fabric and lace. We laugh about the kitchen in the basement and plan our biweekly trip to the pubic bathhouse for showers.

Dan has friends here, most of them single women. I try to do my best to reach out, learn the language, and fit into the culture.

There are chapters in every life
which are seldom read and certainly not aloud.

~ Carol Shields

...I wake up to the baby screaming. *Oh, no, not again.* I pull her cradle next to our bed. *Why doesn't she just sleep?* I am always tired; but worse, I'm in a deep pit of despair. Fear grips me, while Dan turns over and goes back to sleep. I cuddle my perfect newborn girl as a strong and clear feeling falls over me. *Something is desperately wrong. It's a mistake with Dan.*

I chalk it up to postnatal depression. It must be lack of sleep. Dan provides for us by working in the city, gone three to four days at a time. Taking care of our country home, I miss him, but know he is doing what he loves.

...I tuck our three year old into bed and sit down to nurse our newborn. Dan is washing the dishes. Then he sits down with me. I look forward to the evening together. He says he has to go back to the office. His job seems time-consuming and demanding, but when a pastor calls asking him to speak on relationships at a weekend retreat, he takes that on, too. I question him, expressing frustration, but it's brushed off abruptly. He says I'm not letting him be a man. His comebacks are like a slap in the face, but I can't define the feeling. He showers and then gets in the car and drives away.

...We spend our first night in a new house. Early in the morning, nausea sweeps over me. I know this sensation. My period is late. At breakfast, I tell Dan, "I'm pregnant. I'm sure of it."

He is angry. "It's your fault. Why did you let this happen?"

I am stunned. By the third pregnancy—but more by Dan's reaction.

> *If suffering alone taught,*
> *all the world would be wise, since everyone suffers.*
> *To suffering must be added*
> *mourning, understanding, patience, love, openness*
> *and the willingness to remain vulnerable.*
>
> ~ Anne Morrow Lindbergh

...Between his work and speaking engagements, Dan seems preoccupied and isn't home much. I read a slew of books. "If you and your spouse aren't growing together," they say, "you're growing apart." I tell him how I feel and ask, "Why don't you love me?"

"Your expectations are too big," he says.

We hear a sermon on marriage, and one line hits me: "If you aren't making love to your spouse at least once a week, you're too busy."

Why doesn't he hear this? I wonder.

…"I need you to plan a special occasion for our tenth anniversary," I say. "Somewhere nice." It sounds like a demand, but it's my way of saying, *I'm desperate for your affection.*

I juggle three small children and a part-time job, but I need to know—either he cares or he doesn't.

Dan plans a weekend trip—in connection with business. He books a cheap flight and a cheaper hotel room. He isn't present emotionally. We spend the first night arguing. *Why is our marriage so difficult?* I keep asking myself.

…Dan blames our tensions on his job. We decide to move and start over. I support us in sales while he starts a business.

"I hate those suits you wear," Dan says as I dress.

"I have to wear these to make a living for us," I tell him. His barbs snag my peace of mind. But he seems happy to spend the money I make on things we couldn't afford before.

…During the day, Dan works from our home. Evenings, he finds justification to see the "soccer match" at a pub downtown, meet "friends," or take a "photography safari." I wait up for him night after night, always crawling into our empty bed with an eerie ache.

"Give me space," he says when I ask why he avoids me. I blame it on his midlife crisis, his waning business, and my success.

…"I'll be in the city all weekend working on a project," Dan informs me.

"Again? Why?" I counter. His two-day trips to a metropolitan area are increasing. "Can't you just do the research here?"

I feel uneasy about the reasons he gives me.

*You did the best you could according to what you knew.
And when you knew better, you did better.*

∼ Oprah Winfrey

…"There's a late fee on your family account," the video clerk tells me. He reads the name of a movie returned late weeks before.

"I don't remember renting that," I say.

"No, I don't think you *would* rent that one," he answers with a wry smile. "But somebody on this account did."

Confused, and embarrassed, I pay the fee and leave quickly.

…"Don't worry about the kids. Have fun," Dan says. He seems delighted each time I leave on a business trip. I'm proud of the way he jumps in and takes care of the house and girls. He seems proud of me and my job. I never worry about things when I go away.

But this time, I wake up in my hotel room the first night and feel a strong presence in the room. I don't often get on my knees, but this time I do. For several hours, I pour out my heart, compelled to pray for our marriage. I feel God is doing something good at last.

…Home again after an exciting ten-day trip to Israel, I can't wait to see my family and tell them about it. I believe things will be different with Dan and me. But he isn't at the airport to meet me. Half an hour later, he arrives, acting as if nothing is wrong. I'm in tears. He belittles me in front of our girls, blaming me for upsetting them.

Two days later, when we host a dinner party with friends to celebrate that trip to Israel, his attention centers on a certain woman, a neighbor. He keeps pouring drinks for her and leaves "for the office" as soon as she makes her exit.

…Dan is out of town to visit his ailing father. I wake up sweating.

I turn on the light and tell myself it was a nightmare. But my vivid dream of Dan and another woman in an erotic encounter haunts me. In the dream, I asked Dan where he'd been and what he'd done. He sloughed off my suspicions and he lied, not knowing I saw the whole thing.

In real life, when Dan returns home, I confront him with my dream and ask what he was doing while he was gone. He sloughs off my suspicions and shames me for an overactive imagination. I wonder, *Is he right?*

> **The private lie is in our face,**
> **violating the sanctity of our own nest—**
> **the place where we live,**
> **where we let our guard down....**
> **How easily we learn to turn down the volume**
> **on our own inner rumblings—**
> **the ones trying to alert us**
> **that something's going awry.**
>
> ～ Dory Hollander

...For our twentieth wedding anniversary we plan a week-long trip to a romantic destination, though things are difficult between us. One week before we are to leave, Dan tells me we can't afford to go. I'm furious, but I bridle my emotions. I know I'll ruin what little relationship we have if I blow up.

We spend a weekend close to home. Dan doesn't touch me or talk to me on the trip. I confront him with his lack of presence. He says, "I'm fine. I'm here. I'm enjoying myself. Why can't you let me be?"

I feel invisible in black lace.

...Working in the quiet of my home office, I sense a heavy blanket fall over me. I know. *I know* Dan is into pornography on trips to the city and in our home when I'm away.

"Isn't that true?" I ask, when I call him at his office.

Dan sighs. "Yes," he says.

"You need to get counseling," I plead. "Deal with this. Pour out your gut to somebody. Get help."

He agrees.

...Several days later, I find by the bathroom sink a love letter posted from out of town. It's addressed to Dan, alluding to time in bed. When I ask him to explain, he looks both defiant and exposed.

"She didn't really mean this," he says. "You're taking it out of context."

For the first time, I know Dan is lying. This is not an overactive imagination. Truth is there in black and white. He grabs the letter, and leaves.

...After a flurry of phone calls, which Dan always answers, he says finally, "There's something I have to tell you."

I brace myself.

"On my last trip..." He spills out details of an affair with another man's wife—not the person who had written the love letter.

"It didn't mean anything," he says. "She's in love with me now, but I don't love her. I'm cutting the whole thing off."

What is going on? How many are there? I wonder, unable to articulate my despair and his denial. My heart feels like a knife has been plunged into it. *I can't believe this is happening.*

> *Facing reality—*
> *knowing what we know, and knowing*
> *without a shadow of doubt that we know it—*
> *destroys our last shreds of optimism.*
> *There is no turning back.*
>
> *However painful, we're square with the truth;*
> *no use pretending we'll change or he'll change*

or somehow magically, everything will turn out right.
In fact, everything is turning out right.
We can't trade the rawness of reality
for the more muted illusions we once held.
But we can move forward with quiet confidence
that we are holding tightly to the truth.

~ Ellen Sue Stern

…"I'm not going to be depressed anymore," Dan tells me. "I'm leaving."

"Why?" I plead. "We can work this out. I love you. I want to stay married. For us. For the children. I can forgive you. I can change if you want me to. I can meet your needs if I just know what they are: kinky sex, anything."

"No. I've always needed something you're not."

"There's *another* woman?"

"No," he says. "I just have to leave."

I beg Dan to stay just one more week—until our daughter's holiday performance. He agrees.

…"How do I look?" Dan says, a couple days later, giving his body a cool-guy shimmy.

"Whoa," I say. "You look great. Those neat boots! My favorite jeans. You know I love when you dress like that."

Before he leaves, Dan wants to know if I'll be busy all day. "Oh, by the way," he adds, "my work phone is out of order." The next day is the same: cool clothes, phone out of order, "Will you be busy?" And the next. Finally, I demand, "What's going on?" Dan names a certain woman, a neighbor. The Neighbor. "I've been in love with her for five years," he says through phony tears. "She's my soul mate."

He didn't have to tell me the rest.

…Weeks later, Dan and I talk about how to tell our oldest daughter about our breakup; she's spending a semester abroad. I look straight into Dan's eyes and say, "And I know about all your prostitutes and old girlfriends." *I can't believe I said that.*

Dan glares at me. "Have you been talking to my counselor?"

"No," I say, shocked by the truth of my insight.

Numbness envelopes me as Dan admits infidelity starting with our first year of marriage. "I had to do it," he says, insisting it didn't involve intercourse and adding, "I'm still a Christian." He leaves. I stay at my bedside for hours, stunned, immobile.

The best thing about the future
is that it comes only one day at a time.

~ Abraham Lincoln

…A year before Dan left, I had christened the new year "A Year of Light." I wrote my prayer requests, including skylights for our home, in my journal. Little did I realize then how my prayer for light would be answered. Not in the way I expected! Exposure brought nauseating waves of pain and rage. My childhood dream to dance stories on a beautiful stage burst like a bubble. And that kindergarten doll house? Someone else did come and move things around despite the fact that I was there first.

I crawled, trudged, and climbed through that year. I determined to feel the deep rage deeply, then leave it behind. Out of sheer will to survive, I forgave—in increments. I learned to look deeper and harder and to own the truth, no matter how painful. Today I know truth is worth clinging to because it set me free.

This morning an acquaintance told me she's moving across the street from me. I'd seen her eyes swollen recently, the way mine looked last year. I said, "Look, if you're going through what I've just been through, I am so sorry."

She said, "Well, how are you doing?"

"Oh, so much better," I told her.

She sighed with relief and said, "That's what I need to hear."

When I am here for others going the same direction, my own

healing flows—a window through which I recognize that good comes knotted with bad and that joy is tangled up with pain. Accepting that has made me stronger and happier. The negatives continue to develop. Instead of dancing stories on stage, I'm using paper and pen.

Everything in your life is on time. Even this.
Don't hurry the future.

Live the present. Even embrace your pain.
God will heal the past as you move forward
one baby step at a time.

∾ Noelle

4

I Have God
And Me

The way of the good person is like the light of dawn.
It grows brighter and brighter until it is full daylight.
But the wicked are like those who stumble in the dark.
They can't even see what has hurt them.

~ Proverbs 4:18, NCV

K: An old sequoia tree sprawls beside the trail at Calavaras Big Trees State Park two hours from my home. It had fallen before the grove was discovered in 1852.

I noticed it on a hike one day and marveled at the tree's dimensions: seventeen feet in diameter and three hundred feet long. It was hollow, like a tunnel. *Hey, this would provide shelter on a windy day!* I thought. *And what a safe place to spend a stormy night.*

I stepped through the opening. Ribbons of sunlight fell across charred splotches on the inside walls. "Fire-scarred," park rangers describe it. *Had the tree survived a forest fire? Or had people stopped for shelter and built a fire to warm themselves through a dark, cold night?*

The dark and cold—that's what I remember most about the first months of my divorce. *Will I ever find light and warmth?* I wondered then. I was stumbling in the dark while Ed seemed to be getting on with what he wanted, full speed ahead.

I found shelter, but not as I expected. Not in powerful revelations from God, but in the promise of His presence. It wasn't by being rescued by Him financially or by another man emotionally. A smooth road drenched in bright sunlight didn't suddenly appear. I found shelter in the very center of my life's tragedy, a marriage disintegrated from within like a tree weakened by rot that had fallen in disgrace.

I wasn't the first to crawl into the cavern of a hollow tree and build a fire there for warmth and light. I won't be the last. But it took getting past the trauma of being lost and losing myself. In a complex series of events never asked for or expected, I noticed my path growing brighter as I moved ahead, lit by glowing embers from that early fire.

> *The loss of love is a terrible thing.*
> *They lie who say that death is worse.*
>
> ∼ Countee Cullen

This Isn't How I Planned My Life

The dissolution of marriage is not a single legal event. It's a multi-faceted emotional process "more destabilizing and wrenching than any other emotional crisis, including death," claims psychotherapist Joan Rossman, in practice twenty years.[1]

"Divorce," says Helen Richards, a World War II concentration camp survivor, "was worse than Dachau had ever been. In the camp, I was young. It was not a personal thing. There was everybody else. I wanted to survive. But during my divorce, I wanted to die."

Richards, interviewed by Dr. James Dobson, says, "We had been married twenty-four years. I was afraid. I hurt. There was no place to go to hide. Nobody could understand what I felt."[2]

For many Christians, divorce includes personal shame, guilt, feelings of failing God and the church. Still, even within the evangelical community, divorce rates do not differ from society at large.[3] The question arises: To what degree does church teaching on the sacrament of marriage help heal and head off broken families?

Dr. Neal Clark Warren, psychologist, marriage counselor, and author of *The Triumphant Marriage*, says, "I've come to believe that 75 percent of all divorces involve marriages in which at least one partner is emotionally unhealthy." He adds, "Marriages can't cure individual emotional problems."[4]

Neither can the church. Or a healthy partner, no matter how much she would like to or tries. If the unhealthy individual is not willing to own the problem, confess it, or seek personal restoration, the marriage is headed for disaster.

Patterns in the *When He Leaves* scenario are becoming obvious since we began this project and started connecting with other women going through the same thing. We even coined the term *The Neighbor* because most of us seem to have one. Although each divorce is slightly different, there are few surprises. We began to wonder, *Why do these guys, who believe they've met the love of their lives, think they are original? Is there a book for Christian men on how to cheat successfully for twenty-plus years?* Not that we know of.

But, as our book went to the editor, title intact, another hit the bookstores: *Should You Leave?* by best-selling author and psychiatrist Peter Kramer. Kramer's educated diagnosis of the male-leaving phenomenon is uncanny in its insightful validation of our stories. Intended to spare men, their wives, and their children years of pain, he discusses a man's sad unwillingness to entertain the possibility that the problem might be within himself.

In a section on the "woman down the street," Kramer says, "I know this neighbor. Calling her *Carmen*, he says, "Though she is no Gypsy—actually she…has lived for years in the same suburban house…[she] likes action, complications, intrigue, attached men. Once your family turmoil is resolved and you are out in the cold, you will not last a month with her. When you say you need Carmen…you are saying that your hedonic capacity is turned way down low so that it takes enormous stimulation to move you at all. We know that older men need younger women not because the men still have it but because they don't."

The husband will attend counseling, Kramer says, "not because he expects the sessions to be of any use but out of a formal obligation to the wife" and "though you will never admit it, you feel unworthy of your wife, and less capable.…" His thesis reaches a crescendo when he asks, "And what are we to make of your readiness to withdraw from contact with your children, whom you say you adore? The truth is, you can no longer feel pleasure in any sphere."[5]

The larger picture eventually shows that these men lose. We only wonder why they are the last to realize it. Not out to incriminate them, we wish them recovery of self; they have suffered, too. We are here to say to women who must regroup, forge on.

> Since 1900 the divorce rate in the United States rose from 0.7 per 1000 people to 4.8 per 1000 people in 1992. Today, there are 1.2 million divorces each year.[6]
>
> A study based on 352 divorced women across the country indicates one in four marriages will terminate in a midlife divorce. Author and gerontologist Christopher Hayes says the average length of marriage is twenty-three years.[7]
>
> The United States Census Bureau reports that divorce is on the rise among older women.[8]
>
> Gail Sheehy, author of *New Passages: Mapping Your Life Across Time*, says, "Divorce is occurring with greater frequency among people aged 40 to 54. The number of women in that age group surged from 1.5 million in 1970 to 6.1 million in 1991."[9]

The longer you've been married, the more difficulty you may experience going through a divorce. But no matter how many years you were married, when he leaves and the shock begins to wear off, you face:

- intense emotions, including grief, guilt, anger, hopelessness
- stress-related health problems
- disappointment with friends, family, church, and God
- upheaval of financial stability, social context, and family issues
- a deep sense of failure, humiliation, and rejection

How will you survive the emotional roller coaster, let alone rebuild your life? You will survive and move on because:

- when you feel, you heal. You are an integrated human being. Spiritual, mental, and emotional healing will facilitate physical well-being.

- you are on a journey discovering what is real and what is not. "And you shall know the truth, and the truth shall make you free"(Jn. 8:32).

- you will learn a new skill we call turnabout thinking. It will change all the "d-i-s's" and "d-e-s's" in your life (disappointment, disillusionment, disarray, despair, desertion, despondency) to building blocks for a brand new you.

Are You Going Crazy?

The specific losses of divorce and each woman's reaction to them are individual. Here are a few issues the two of us faced differently.

Faith

N: When a friend told me her divorce helped her grow because her faith in God went from zero to 100 percent, I told her, "Well, my faith went from 100 percent to zero. Everything I've ever believed will have to be rebuilt from the ground up." Rebuilding was a painstaking and tenuous process.

> **Blessed are those whose dreams are shaped by their hopes and not by their hurts.**
>
> ～ Robert Schuller

K: My faith stayed intact and helped me through. In joint counseling before, during, and after our seven-month separation, I poured my heart out while Ed sat in stoic silence.

This was two years before the divorce. I can still see him, just home from one of the sessions, standing beside the freezer in the garage: "You and your faith," he accused. "You are always so Goody Two-shoes." With strength that was not mine, I stepped toward him. "Don't you ever—ever again attack my faith in God," I said.

> Prisoner-of-war accounts indicate that some POWs may die for no apparent reason other than a loss of hope. Hope means simply the belief that something good lies ahead. It is not the same as optimism or wishful thinking, for these imply a denial of reality....Realistic hope permits a dying person to confront reality, but at the same time gives strength to go on living.[10]
>
> Philip Yancey

The Family Home

N: I kept my home, working out an arrangement for payment with Dan, who respected my boundaries there. But living in the same small town not far from him and only a few streets from The Neighbor was painful. Friends asked, "How can you do it? Don't you want to move? Won't you have to in order to survive?"

My stubbornness came to the rescue. "This is my home," I countered. "This is my town, my place. I did nothing wrong. I can hold my head high. I'm staying." It was very hard for a long time. Finally, the girlfriend moved and became someone else's neighbor.

Better is a dry morsel with quietness, Than a house full of feasting with strife.

~ Proverbs 17:1

K: Our family home had to be sold. Before it closed escrow, Ed moved out; but he came and went unannounced, whether I was home or at work, until I changed the locks.

"This is my home now," I told him. "We need ground rules we both understand. I'd appreciate it if you would not be in the house without me present, just as I'm not in your home. And please call before you come."

After I moved into a home of my own, my physical and emotional safety became top priority. I needed Melanie's cooperation to ensure that my personal boundaries and our joint privacy were not violated. She had to sit alone in the garage after school a few times until she promised not to let her dad inside when I wasn't there. When she threatened to go live with him because I had "only one bath and lousy green carpet," I endured her complaints.

> Divorce often keeps you living at the burial site of your marriage. The primary reasons are children, job, support systems and family ties....If you have children, moving [to another area] is virtually impossible because the courts recognize the need for the other parent to be physically present in your children's lives. Moving with children usually demands the other parent's permission. We all need fresh starts and new beginnings after a crisis. It may mean that you can only move across town rather than across the country.[11]
>
> Jim Smoke

Sexual Trauma

N: I was devastated by the revelation of my Christian husband's infidelities. I struggled with issues of femininity and sensuality. Why hadn't he desired me? Wasn't I good enough? How could I have been so blind, accepting his explanations when I was sometimes suspicious? What were the needs he now claimed I wasn't meeting? Would any other man love and desire me?

I was brokenhearted. But I met others going through the same thing who were coping with STDs and the fear of AIDS. My counselor explained sexual addictions and the pathological lying that accompanies them. She urged me not to believe his claims of abstinence and no penetration; I needed to be tested. I hadn't believed him anyway, but going in for those tests was the ultimate degradation. It took a long time to get up the nerve.

The man I loved had taken advantage of my innocence, virginity, and submission. He, of all people, knew how much I prized my health and our sexual relationship. Who knew how many people I had been coupled with through his lifestyle? It took a long time to realize his lying extended beyond covering his tracks and the things he told me. In order to validate his dissipated masculinity, he had to believe the lies himself.

> *The orgasm has replaced the cross as the focus*
> *of longing and the image of fulfillment.*
>
> ∼ Malcolm Muggeridge

K: Ed changed when I became a mother. He started accusing me of "not meeting his needs." But when I asked what they were, he didn't know. Over the years, I purchased slinky negligees and planned a vacation to Hawaii; but the first thing he hit on was the TV remote. I felt immobilized and depressed by his avoidance—exactly where he wanted me! A month after he filed for divorce, I requested an AIDS test because I was suspicious, but I had no substantial proof of infidelities. That night I wrote my first journal entry: "Jesus, my example...uttered no threats...but kept entrusting Himself to Him who judges righteously" (see 1 Pet. 2:21-24). When I learned of Ed's affairs, I was both humiliated and furious. Media coverage of the AIDS crisis shook my core and still does. I had felt "safe," since he was the only man I'd slept with.

Eventually, I met The Neighbor. She apologized. I said I'd try to forgive her. Together, we matched the "business trips" with "the rendezvous" and pieced Ed's excuses with reality. She had no idea she was one of his many "other women." At last, I realized Ed had a big problem and that it wasn't me.

> Christian marriage rests upon more than an initial covenant; it rests upon the fidelity of each spouse to the other....'What God has joined together....' Adultery, upon which we tend to place such singular emphasis, represents an external [visible] breach.... An internal [invisible] breach in thought or attitude can also break the covenant. It is known only to the one who is secretly pulling away. But if left to continue the process becomes irreversible in time, except for God's intervention. Covenant unity can be broken because one or both spouses walk away from its obligations or turn off mentally or emotion-ally....Whenever a spouse is aware of being no longer commit-ted to covenant goals or obligations, to marital unity as total partnership or to a loving mutuality, then the covenant is beginning to come apart. Sexual infidelity then is symptom, not cause. Divorce then merely gives decent burial to the marriage that died—or was murdered![12]
>
> Dwight Small

Financial Stress

W: Just prior to Dan's leaving, I lost my job and most of my friends when the company I worked for moved out of state. I started to freelance, but the decision to do that had been based on Dan's moral support. Now, emotionally traumatized and alone, I found it hard to produce. When I barely got my feet under me, he said he couldn't make child-support payments as per our agreement. I realized it's never over—even post divorce.

I envied friends who were well set up, but told Dan, "Fine. Default. I'll make it anyway." I traded my used car for a cheaper model with better mileage, borrowed on life insurance, and used my credit card for groceries. Friends told me, "Don't be too proud to receive." Family members found ways to offer help—a load of wood or gifts they knew the children needed.

I did something I'd never done before: prayed for money, lots of it. I worked and waited. At times God's silence was deafening. My work came through, and Dan missed only one payment. That month I got an unexpected reimbursement from a company in just the amount I was short. Very slowly I began to edge forward.

Better is a dinner of herbs where love is,
Than a fatted calf with hatred.

∽ Proverbs 15:17

K: I was self-employed, without the security of a salary or health, disability, or vacation benefits. Being on call at three different firms meant I seldom knew before six o'clock each evening whether I had a job the next day. I drove over one hundred miles a day; gas and car repairs were a big expense. I managed to support my daughter on what I made, plus minimal child support.

I had no time or energy for games, such as when Ed handed me a year's worth of predated checks and three months later canceled the account. I knew if I were tied up in the legal system I would miss time from work, lose income, and spend more money on attorney and accountant fees than I would ever collect from Ed. I determined to show him that I didn't need him or his child-support checks and adjusted my standard of living accordingly. I kept hearing, *Let go and I will bless you,* through the advice of my attorney, my pastor, and my parents, and through my devotional reading. That didn't mean God removed my financial needs, but He helped me meet them.

Individual Priorities

N: We didn't think twice about keeping our dog, Puppsie, because he was almost like one of the children. But we did begin to economize, excluding luxuries like soda pop and red meat from the larder and making fewer trips to the store—any store. Clothes, dental checkups, and movies were out of the question for a long time.

> **For where your treasure is,**
> **there your heart will be also.**
>
> ∼ Matthew 6:21

K: When a representative from Pets-In-Need drove off with our dog, Rebby, I was devastated. But I couldn't afford to keep her and our cat, Cindy, too. After I found out the rep was the widow of my favorite doctor, I took it as a positive sign Rebby was in good hands. Ed played off my guilt by telling Melanie how cruel I was to get rid of her dog. She didn't understand I had no choice. I felt awful.

Let's Face It!

According to Carol Ryff, well-being is the presence of six life qualities:

- independence
- the ability to cope with complex demands
- feeling of growth as a person
- good relationships
- goals that give life meaning
- an acceptance of the self and the past[13]

Divorce forces you to face these six life qualities. When you get on the other side, you realize waves of anxiety, anger, and regret inundate you from time to time; but if you think about it, your fears aren't much different from other people's in today's changing, unpredictable world. Others are scared, too—about losing their jobs, growing old, being alone. They have regrets about wasting their youth and not spending enough time with their children.

Divorce makes you face your vulnerability sooner, as would a chronic disease or a disability. In facing vulnerability, you become more reachable and transparent.

As a Christian woman, perhaps you were taught vulnerability and transparency were not good. You were taught to keep your personal concerns to yourself. As one 1927 book put it: "It is women's duty to fill the home with sunshine and cheer…like a chirping bird." As you allow yourself to be transparent through crisis, you will realize how appropriate, how very positive and healing it is to be who you are.

> *The best remedy for a bruised heart, is not,*
> *as some people seem to think,*
> *repose upon a manly bosom.*
> *Much more efficacious are honest work,*
> *physical activity, and the sudden acquisition of wealth.*
>
> ∾ Dorothy L. Sayers

K: In my home, a one-of-a-kind vase is perched on a shelf. I bought a similar one for Noelle. They're fashioned from sections of seventy-year-old juniper fence posts found in Montana. In the hands of artist John Noyes, the top part of each vase has been sanded smooth, revealing fine swirling colors of rust and gold. A glass vial was inserted to hold a sprig of wild flowers. The bottom half remains in its distressed form—rugged, grey, knotted, gnarled, pierced with a rusty nail or two.

From a living, breathing tree, to a fallen log, to weathered fence posts, to vases, the raw material found service and beauty. And in the creative hands of a loving God, so will you.

P. S. You'll see.

5

My Hope
Is Increasing

For by You I can run against a troop;
By my God I can leap over a wall.
As for God, His way is perfect;
The word of the LORD is proven;
He is a shield to all who trust in Him.

~ 2 Samuel 22:30, 31

N: I love the picture by artist Mary Englebreit of the woman sitting in a rocker, patching up a torn and ragged heart. The view from her window shows a winding trail to the horizon. But her attention is focused on the important thing right in her lap.

In mending, my first instinct was to protect the hurt muscle from further injury. I couldn't rush emotional healing just as a doctor can't hurry the healing of a broken bone. Instead, the doctor immobilizes it in a cast; given time and protection, it will heal itself.

Sometimes I just sat and rocked the reality of my divorce: wailing or whimpering. My tears cleansed and softened the wound. When I allowed myself to feel my feelings, not demanding too much too soon, I was doing something nice for myself.

What I remember most about those first months was the waiting—waiting for something good to happen and wondering if it ever would. But while rocking, I discovered simple tools to craft strong, even decorative, stitches in the heart: the beautifully colored threads of friendship. Sharp scissors to snip away frayed edges, snags, and dead ends. Needles in different sizes to accommodate the always-changing fabric of my life.

What really broke a heart was taking away its dream.

∽ Pearl Buck

When the Dream Dies

Divorce is learning to live in serenity with your losses. Experts say that under normal circumstances a person's energy is distributed equally in four areas: spiritual, physical, mental, and emotional. During divorce, 85 percent of your energy goes to emotional coping. The remaining 15 percent goes to the other areas combined. That's why, running low on spiritual energy, you have trouble praying; low on mental energy, you have trouble concentrating; low on physical energy, you feel exhausted.

You go through the motions, the practical steps: the lawyers' meetings, the settlement agreement, the packing, the furniture moving, the final decree. Then out of nowhere, when you think you are finally getting somewhere, you remember the little girl whose dreams were ripped off.

So be kind to yourself as you mend and patch. Your broken heart is drawing almost all your energy right now. Don't be embarrassed by scar tissue. In time, it leaves the skin stronger and shows you've been through something you somehow wish you hadn't and yet are rather proud you have been.

K: I shut the garage door and backed my car out of the driveway into the street. The sun dipped low on the horizon, drenching the house in a purple-pinkish glow. Yellow daffodils danced along the front walkway of our family home, the one I was leaving forever.

My eyes scanned the plastic bags and boxes awaiting charity pickup along the front porch. They bulged with odds and ends I no longer had room to store. At first I thought, *I'm seeing things.* One of the bag seams had torn. Taffeta and lace spilled out and flapped in the breeze. *This is the way a marriage ends,* I thought. *The skirt of my wedding dress is waving good-bye.*

A woman's tender heart bleeds when soaked with rejection.

∼ Kari

N: I forced my legs to carry me up the stairs to Dan's new apartment, though I didn't want to see him or his new place. The evening was cold, and snow lay in small drifts against the steps. I was lugging the last of his things from our home: a couple screwdrivers, a box of assorted screws, and the wall plugs he'd asked for.

Dan stepped outside the door, and I caught a glimpse of a painting leaning against the wall inside, the one he'd proudly given me on one of our anniversaries. He invited me in to see the secondhand bed he'd just repainted and antiqued; but I declined, not wanting to imagine who was going to sleep in it with him. I handed over the things.

This is the way a marriage ends, I thought.

Where Reality Begins

Death of a marriage is not the end of the line. You think, *He got it the way he wanted.* Even if he did, his way is not the final say-so; divorce is not the last word. If you dare, there are new directions. There are choices somewhere between wallowing in misery or going off like a fool and dreaming again.

C.S. Lewis said, "Of course, we never wanted, and never asked, to be made into the sort of creatures He is going to make us into....We must not be surprised if we are in for a rough time....God is forcing [us] on,...putting [us] into situations where [we] will have to be very much braver, or more patient, or more loving, than [we] ever dreamed of being before.[1] Where the old dream ends, a new one can begin. Only you can do the necessary heart work.

Great faith isn't the ability to believe long and far into the misty future.
It's simply taking God at His word and taking the next step.

~ Joni Eareckson Tada

K ● "Don't change your tender heart and become vindictive," said Barney, a friend since high school. "Somebody out there is looking for someone just like you."

Barney was right. God used rejection to recycle, renew, and redirect my focus. I now write about hope and purpose, serve in our church divorce-recovery ministry, and guess what?

I married a man who accepts me just as I am.

If we go down into ourselves,
we find that we possess exactly what we desire.

∼ Simone Weil

N ● "I can't be divorced," I told my counselor early on. "I'm not made that way. I can't be a single mom." But God (with my cooperation) began to create a quilt out of the remnants of my life. Little by little, I started enjoying what I could do, inviting friends over to fill our house, and planning new ways to make memories.

I still can't believe it—a new person is emerging. The new me is less straight, less stressed, and more free. I still quake at life's unknowns, but an oppression has lifted that I was unaware of until, with distance, I realized it was no longer there.

Heart Work Is Individual

Someday you, too, will look beyond the window and say, "I love where I'm heading." But for now, your attention is focused on the heart work lying in your lap. Threading the needle that will pierce the fabric and prick your finger. Recycling what's ragged and worn into an heirloom.

Spiritual Renewal

K • I tended to take on more than I could handle. Sometimes my pulse raced over 160—sitting. I kept tripping over Psalm 46:10: "Be still, and know that I am God." *And just how do I "be still" with too much to do and so much to process?* I wondered.

I discovered it meant swinging just one foot at a time off the edge of the bed instead of mindless rushing. Early on, when my anger came quickly and was automatic, I determined to forgive Ed. I wanted to live my values and vision in stillness. The Lord's return gave me something to look forward to. I knew that when I stand in heaven, God won't look me over for accomplishments like a fifty-year marriage; He'll be interested in whether I stayed faithful to Him.

Recently, I found a slip of paper in a file from that time. It reads, "The kind of faith God values seems to develop best when everything fuzzes over, when God stays silent, when the fog rolls in.... Fidelity involves learning to trust that, out beyond the perimeter of fog, God still reigns and has not abandoned us, no matter how it may appear." [2]

N • At first, I couldn't pray at all. My father kept reminding me: "God didn't fail you, Noelle. Dan failed God." Later, I dressed my wounds with a short and simple liturgy I wrote myself and prayed every single morning: "Lord, take my broken pieces. That's all I have. Rearrange and put them back together in a new paradigm." I'm still praying that prayer, changing the prayers I tag onto it:

- *An affirmation:* "I love and accept you just the way you are. I welcome happiness, love, intimacy, and prosperity into your life."

- *A homespun cry:* "Eternal Father, help me keep a clean conscience. I want to move beyond my hate."

I examined my life for failures and sins of omission in my marriage. It was hard. I was self-righteous. I'm not sure I'm through. I ask the Lord to show me and forgive me, then help me look deeper. When faith appears to fail, I make room for disappointment and let spiritual questions rise to the surface.

> *But may the God of all grace,*
> *who called us to His eternal glory by Christ Jesus,*
> *after you have suffered a while,*
> *perfect, establish, strengthen, and settle you.*
>
> ~ 1 Peter 5:10

Emotional Refocus

K. I learned to live the moments before I made it through the months. In time, I discovered the peace that comes from holding everything and everyone around me loosely. I had to let go.

- *Being Ed's wife.* I thought at first that it was better than being alone. Divorced, I no longer fit in our couples' Sunday School class or with friends at a dinner table for six. I couldn't check *married* on official documents, conveying stability to the business world. But when I untangled my feelings, I knew I would be okay on my own.

- *Our special place.* Ed and I spent many weekends clearing the lot and fixing up our mountain cabin. We dreamed of retiring there, someday uniting our frantic lives. Now things are different. Richard is in my life. We live in the Bay Area with Melanie, four dogs, and two goats. I walk through our wild-flower garden, scattering birdseed. As I watch it cascade across the wrinkled knees of the hillside, I think, *Live one day at a time. Hold it close, then let it go.*

- *The privacy of my emotions and stability of my values.* I felt exposed when the divorce summons arrived in the mail with my name on it. That meant a file documenting the end of my marriage was in the county clerk's office, open to the public. And instead of the newspaper announcing my twenty-fifth wedding anniversary, a divorce notice silently screamed: *Failure. And you call yourself a Christian?*

At first, I questioned what I believed about myself. Was I too serious? unattractive? unlovable? Should I slap on more makeup or lighten my hair? study how-to-flirt books? hit the bar scene?

Instead, I went looking for God and found the "right-now" way of looking at His assurances. I bathed my mind in the Psalms. And when Melanie spent weekends with Ed, I learned to relish a quiet, empty house as I stretched out on the couch with a book and classical music. I said, "Yes. I am content at this moment."

I determined that only God could redeem and stabilize my life. I decided to believe He would because He loves me and treasures a pure heart, a gentle spirit, and honesty. I faced my fear of public humiliation and shame by talking about divorce to friends and family. Each time I encountered another divorcee, I felt her anguish and sometimes I hugged her.

N: As a divorcee-to-be, I cried the entire first two meetings in my recovery group. My wound was raw. I felt I'd had the worst experience of anyone, until a young woman joined who'd just found out her best friend's baby had been fathered by her soon-to-be-ex-husband. Before, I would have thought, "How do people get themselves in messes like that?" Now, I knew humiliation like that can come out of nowhere.

In my first efforts to rise above my own pain, I told myself: *Get out of bed. Kiss the children. Buy milk.* Next: *Cry when you feel like it. Think beautiful. Make room for whimsy.* But it got harder. I

A PRAYER FOR RAGE

by Richard Foster[3]

~ Acknowledgment:

Dear God, I come to you with an overwhelming anger, a bursting rage. This rage is like a cancer shut up in my bones eating away at my soul. Today, O God, I acknowledge this rage. I do not suppress it or hide from it. Thank you, Lord, for accepting me, rage and all.

~ Expression:

O God, I feel a burning rage within, a fire gone wild, burning, always burning. God, I hate what was done to me. It was so evil. So wrong. Why this evil? Why this degradation? Why? Why? Why? My rage, O God, is the only power I have against this vicious world. That's why I cannot let it go. Please, God, don't ask me to let it go.

~ Turning:

God, I cannot separate my hatred for what was done from the person who did it. I despise the deed. I loathe the person who did the deed. My rage is my only revenge. But, God, my rage destroys me, too. I feel this seething anger searing my own soul. O Lord, my God, deliver me from the evil I would do to myself.

wanted to allow love a place, so I faced down destructive thought patterns. To break the cycle of hateful thoughts engulfing me, I learned to change the way I felt about the bad things.

I set a goal to see the truth, not the lies, in what happened. Instead of allowing myself to think, *Betrayed. Ripped off. Trashed,* I trained myself to view things from a larger perspective. The Neighbor did me a favor by forcing Dan's infidelities into the light. *He* lost the precious things: a good wife, a beautiful home, and his family.

My negative emotions toward him eventually neutralized. I no longer feel hate or love. Perhaps with time I'll feel friendly. I rest in the fact there is a time for everything and I don't have to force it. I have a right to emotional boundaries while I'm healing.

> *You don't know where*
> *the wind will blow....*
> *In the same way...*
> *you can't understand what*
> *[God] is doing.*
> *Begin planting*
> *early in the morning,*
> *and don't stop working*
> *until evening....*
> *You don't know which things you*
> *do will succeed.*
> *It is even possible that everything*
> *you do will succeed.*

~ Ecclesiastes 11:5, 6, NCV

Practical Recycle

K. Accepting my new role was a critical decision. I risked turning corners and embracing a changing me. I found I could do:

- Simple things I'd never tried before. Caulking the bathtub, pouring concrete in driveway cracks, painting the fence, and climbing on the roof to inspect shingles. I was rewarded with the pride of accomplishment.

- Big things I'd never done before. I handled insurance paperwork after an automobile accident, including estimates, repairs, and car rental; qualified for a mortgage; and purchased my own home.

- Incredible things I'd never imagined. Ignoring Ed's harassing letters and phone calls, responding in a strictly business fashion. Giving up my right to vindicate myself when I heard what he was saying about me. "Truth needs no defense," I told myself and others, deciding other people would believe what they wanted and I would waste energy trying to change their opinion.

- Beautiful things with so little. Remodeling memories, I splashed my home with light and color—peachy tones and splotches of apple green

∼ Forgiving:

I refuse to allow this evil to control me anymore. I will not be held in bondage to my hate any longer. But the strength to love is not in me. I must wait for your enabling. Now in your great power and with a trembling heart I speak your word of forgiveness.

∼ Healing:

May your healing light shine, O God, into every crack and crevice of my soul. Rage once made me feel strong. But now I receive your light, encircling me with love. I have not forgotten what was done to me. I will never forget. But today, I choose to live as your child of infinite worth.

Amen

ALL THE COMFORTS
OF HOME

Tuck seasonal indulgences into your lifestyle:

∽ Summer:

• *Grow mint in a pot. Use it in salads, ice teas, and lemonade. Freeze it in ice cubes for stews, marinades, and hot teas in winter.*

• *Use a sunscreen and relax outside for a few minutes each day. Listen for summer sounds and smells, and write them in your journal.*

• *Take down heavy drapes and decorations and for a change, enjoy the white space in your home.*

∽ Autumn:

• *By the fireside, go on a seed-catalog tour for bulbs that help you envision color next spring. Take a mug of hot apple cider with you.*

• *Bundle up and let your hair down—stroll along the beach or in the park on a windy day.*

• *Join a choir or the circus! This is the season to make new friends.*

and sky blue. Ed was welcome to the black vinyl look he took with him. Instead of crying over the garden I'd lost, I bought two redwood boxes for my patio, planted seeds, picked off snails, and then pampered my home with sweet-scented bouquets.

And I learned I was not alone. The first evening I stood in the doorway of a divorce-recovery class, I felt embarrassed and ashamed. Later, I realized my fears were the same as everyone's in that room. Soon I made friends and started a monthly potluck. I helped with the church single-again group, volunteered for leadership, and became a speaker.

N: I began to accept, even embrace, the changes turning my life upside down—the divorce and my reduced circumstances. I used the momentum of blessing to initiate change. This is what I did:

• painted our front door hunter green.

• hung a shiny brass porch lamp in place of a clunky old black one.

• planted a baby maple tree in my front lawn to mark my passage into a new life.

• redecorated empty spots on the walls with newly framed pictures and photos.

• lost twenty pounds and enjoyed the compliments.

- invested in a good eye cream.
- cleaned out closets and gave fifty bags and boxes to charity.
- took a bunch of clothes to a resale shop and earned enough for two new outfits.
- welcomed an exchange student into our home. Presto, I had four daughters!
- when I started buying shoes again, I went for high heels to give me a lift.

> **Whatever happens**
> **that breaks us open**
> **to a deeper invasion**
> **of the Lord's spirit**
> **is a blessing in disguise.**
> **Whenever we face difficulties**
> **and problems that**
> **break our willfulness**
> **or arrogant control of our lives,**
> **it is a gift.**
>
> ∽ Lloyd John Ogilvie

I Like This New Me

Handmade heirlooms are rich gifts. Whether quilted, crocheted, embroidered, or tatted, every stitch contains a thought. Even strips of threadbare clothing can be braided into a beautifully patterned rug. When your fingers travel across the ridges of Grandmother's afghan neatly folded across your bed, you trace the mind of its creator.

∽ Winter:

- *Invest in a box of scented candles. Light them in the late afternoon and keep them glowing all evening.*
- *Invite a friend for coffee at a place you've never been before.*
- *Make a list of books you want to read and put several on reserve at the library. Take time to read one every three weeks.*

∽ Spring:

- *Rise early and walk a couple miles before breakfast. Look for firsts: the first crocus, the first robin.*
- *Buy the latest nail polish and a new pair of open-toe shoes.*
- *Write a letter to yourself about personal dreams you haven't told anyone. Seal it in a self-addressed, stamped envelope, and give it to a friend, asking her to mail it to you in a year.*

Sò it is with the leftover fabric of your life. God works with the dark and light threads to weave an original. The patterns take on personality as the textures change. The loose, tangled threads will one day be straightened and tucked. In cold nights to come, you will snuggle beneath a legacy of years: scraps of yesterday, squares of today, swatches of tomorrow, safe and warm.

Even on days when you hide under the covers, like the psalmist you can say, "When I awake, I am still with You" (Psalm 139:18).

Are you made of sturdy stuff? Are you creative? inventive? resourceful?

You are all of the above. It is God in you, the hope of glory.

P.S. You're beautiful!

6

I Need
Time to Feel
So I Can Heal

There is a right time for everything:
. . . a time to cry
. . . a time to grieve
. . . a time for scattering stones
. . . a time not to hug
. . . a time to lose
. . . a time to tear
. . . a time to be quiet
. . . a time for hating.

~ Ecclesiastes 3:1-8, TLB

K: "You're from tough pioneer stock," my mother had said as I hopped aboard that westbound train. At eighteen, I'd courageously packed my trunk with well-folded ideals and vivid dreams. In midlife, embarking on singleness again, I lugged the heavy baggage that goes with a divorce—now filled with rumpled ideals and faded dreams.

I wondered, *Will anyone ever love me again, so steeped in anxiety and seething with rage? Was Ed right when he called me crazy and left me?* I digested his rejection like glass, worried about losing what little courage remained. When I needed to focus on a new direction, I couldn't focus at all.

One evening after work, I went back to our former home to pay rent due. I'd lived there after escrow closed while searching for a place of my own. My heart pumped wildly as I walked up the steps and rang the bell. I wrote my check to the new owner, then quickly drove off. It was agonizing to see a different family living there.

Several miles down the road, I felt uneasy. After pulling to the curb, I switched on the dashboard light to double-check my figures. Feeling the stare of every passing motorist, I recalculated and finally arrived at the same total twice. *I've written the check for a couple hundred dollars too much!* Embarrassed, I returned to say I'd made a mistake. I felt humiliated. Annoyed. Vulnerable. *Am I going crazy?*

No. I was going through a divorce.

My mind told me I was an intelligent, stable, responsible woman. But my confidence was sinking. I was physically exhausted and emotionally overwhelmed. I had been spiritually shaken. When I discovered a pile of bank statements pushed to the back of my desk, I admitted I was coming mentally unglued. I felt like the overturned truck and trailer I'd recently seen on a busy highway near my home. Its remains and contents were scattered across the grassy divider.

Had the driver survived? I wondered. *Will I?*

> *Anyone who believes that God guarantees*
> *a successful marriage to every Christian*
> *is in for a shock.*
>
> ∾ Dr. James Dobson

Where Do I Start?

Divorce victims look a lot like that overturned truck and trailer. Upside down. Sprawled across the divider of past and present while curiosity seekers watch from the side. *What happened to your marriage?* they seem to say through a glance or a nod. Few take the initiative to ask, *What is happening to you?* Most are waiting for the scene to be cleaned up and the wreck relegated to the past so everyone can get on with their lives. Some say plainly, "Get over it."

Bewildered, you wonder, *Where do I start?* The landscape before you is littered with the lifeblood of lost love. Only you know how much you have lost: A companion. Family. Your identity as somebody's wife. Hope. Purpose. Friends. Face. Maybe your faith. Only you feel the pain of picking through the fragments. Only you know the agony of walking away from precious things and feeling your mind and body may end up as shattered as your heart.

The degree of shock and numbness you experience depends

upon the severity of your injury. The more the dream meant to you, the closer your attachment, the deeper the wound. The more you invested in the man and the relationship, the heavier your losses. Shock numbs the pain for a while. But shock wears off. Eventually, you feel.

And feel you must. Never be afraid to feel honest emotion, because that is where healing begins.

"Accepting reality translates into a specific skill with predictable physiological and emotional results," says Barbara Lang Stern. "The loss sinks in....Your thoughts are concerned with wanting things to be different and, in response, your brain starts firing messages (which you experience as feelings) that something is wrong."[1]

Quoting Gary Ember, Ph.D., director of the Los Angeles Center for Cognitive Therapy, Stern says, "'As long as you don't accept the messages, your brain keeps sending them to you. Your alternative to resisting reality is to make a conscious decision to accept the existing situation, including the fact that you're distressed by it....' Acceptance is a first step, not a last...."[2]

There are times in life when each of us,
no matter how mature and well, is frankly unglued.
We need to...simply allow ourselves the clumsiness
and awkwardness of being hurt and untogether.

∼ Dr. Alla Renee Bozarth

No Wonder It Hurts So Much

The aftermath of divorce, like debris left behind at an accident scene, is not predictable or uniform. Tear apart a piece of paper. You end up with two uneven, ragged edges. Part of the left side remains with the right side and vice versa. Divorce rips your most intimate spiritual, physical, emotional, and mental bonds. Part of who you are remains with your former spouse, and part of who he is stays with you. No wonder it hurts so much.

When you admit and accept the pain of this separation, you validate the biblical standard for the sanctity and sacrament of marriage: two people becoming *one flesh*. Divorce sounds and smells like torn flesh. No wonder God hates it (Mal. 2:16). He created man in his image, then said, "It is not good that man should be alone" (Gen. 2:18). Marriage represents the relationship between Christ and the church (Eph. 5:23-32). This mystery of attachment created in marriage is one of God's best ideas.

John Townsend, clinical psychologist and former co-director of Minirth-Meier Clinic West claims, "Attachment or bondedness is our deepest need....It means letting others inside the private vulnerable parts of ourselves.... It occurs when we take the risk to allow someone else to matter enough to us to hurt us if they choose to."[3]

Brenda Hunter, author of *Beyond Divorce* says, "Possibly no marital act affects the self-esteem as deeply as having a spouse choose someone else to love. I do not care whether the involvement is emotional or sexual or both. The fact remains that I, the wife, am in some area of my life found wanting....What I valued, what I believed, were obviously insignificant....What I was, was simply not enough."[4]

"Affairs don't just happen," Hunter says, "they are willed into existence. Prior to the affair, there is a deliberate turning away from the spouse and a willful search for another person."[5]

The pain you experience after rejection is a bold message about the fundamental importance of attachment. Many counselors claim healing can take one year for every four years of marriage. But time itself does not restore. Time is a tool God uses to move you through the moments, days, weeks, and years of life. Time is the dimension within which you heal, a gift of room and space where change can occur.

In the beginning, the best choice you make is to choose to accept what has happened to you and embrace it. The pain will not last forever.

At times, when the pain is most intense,
there is nothing but to merely try keeping sane
and alive one more day.
At other times,
when the hurting is not so excruciating,
it actually sharpens the senses.
These are moments for discovering
what otherwise cannot be easily learned.

∾ Author Unknown

N: At first, Dan communicated to his family and friends that our divorce was a mutual agreement and procrastinated filing. Did he want to be able to say I initiated the final split? He alluded to me in front of a witness that he would stay married if I accepted his mistresses.

After we separated, Dan agreed to marriage counseling. During that period he bought a birthday present for The Neighbor on our joint credit card and belittled me for "overreacting" when the fact he slept with her came to light. Our counselor laid a hand on his shoulder. "Dan, you're not giving this a chance," he said. "If you decide to make your marriage work, call, make another appointment, and let's talk about it with Noelle." Dan never called him back.

I had trusted Dan. I had believed in his sincerity. But when his pretense was exposed, my pain quotient went off the chart. He twisted my anger back against me. "There! You see? I can't be married to an angry woman," he said.

But my anger at Dan was nothing compared to the rage I hurled against myself. "How could I have been so naive?" I asked another counselor. "Was I wrong to trust him all these years?"

"No," she replied. "Trust is the gift you are supposed to give your spouse. You did the right thing. The problem was, he wasn't worthy of it."

Little by little I learned that trusting my negative feelings—guilt, anger and sadness—would bring me insight, comfort, and energy as I interpreted their messages.

Anger is such a healthy emotion.
I didn't feel enough of it; so therefore,
I felt more pain as guilt and low self-esteem took over.

∼ Arlene Somerville

Forever Changed

Sometimes you wish you could turn off the feelings. Push a button. Poof! Anger and anguish disappear. You long to escape because it hurts too much. Some nights, the only way you can fall asleep is to daydream yourself into an exotic world where stars are warm on a dark night and ocean foam is like a caressing cashmere blanket.

But morning comes soon enough. In the face of desperation, a kind of raw courage rises to the surface. You realize, *If I weren't angry, then something would be wrong.*

In certain situations, rage may be the only appropriate response. Karl Miller, a marriage and family therapist at Covenant Psychological Services in Redwood City, California, says: "Anger can be used two ways. To separate and get in touch with our boundaries, or as a way to keep the other person involved with us." Miller, a former pastor who remarried after divorce, believes some relationships are hostile-dependent. "Anger is a way to hang on to a relationship," he says.[6]

When you rant, "How could you do this to me?" it may prevent you from detaching emotionally. Okay, you make mistakes expressing rage. Don't beat yourself up. You rage because you loved. In the sinkholes of destructive emotions, a higher love can fan flames of forgiveness. You will learn ways to allow this fire to empower you. How? Do you pretend it will go away? kick the dog? shop it off? blame yourself, then reach for the cookie jar? decide all men are jerks? How do you detach without losing more of yourself in the process?

Archibald Hart, former dean of the Graduate School of Psychology and professor at Fuller Theological Seminary in Pasadena, California, says to confront painful feelings and move beyond them.[7]

Giving yourself permission to feel love, then anger and each emotion in between, may appear to spiral you backward and downward. It doesn't. To feel is to be alive. Feelings help you live rooted in the here and now and remember why you got here. Pain provides clues of truth as you peel away the layers of loss. Feelings make you human. Feelings also make you more like Christ.

"God used Hosea's unhappy story to illustrate his own whip-saw emotions," writes Philip Yancey. ". . . As Israel broke his trust again and again, he was forced to endure the awful shame of a wounded lover." Yancey says God's tone is close to self-pity: "I am like a moth to Ephraim, like rot to the people of Judah."

Yancey continues: "God seems to 'change his mind' every few seconds....He is preparing to obliterate Israel—wait, now he is weeping, holding out open arms—no, he is sternly pronouncing judgment again. These shifting moods seem hopelessly irrational except to anyone who has been jilted by a lover."[8]

Divorce Changes How You Look at Life:

- You lose your innocence but gain discernment.
- You learn when you feel, you heal.
- You realize rejection cannot define you, unless you allow it.
- You accept that reality sometimes hurts like crazy but sets you free.

Talk About Tears

Our Creator made us, in his wisdom and in his image, with the capacity for love, anger, and jealousy; joy, sadness, and hurt. He respects these emotions. The psalmist exclaimed, "A broken...heart—These, O God, You will not despise (Ps. 51:17).

Jesus promised, "Blessed are those who mourn" (Matt. 5:4). Mark 15:37 records Christ's last excruciating breath was preceded by a loud cry.

God built healing right into heartbreak. He created tear ducts so we can weep. William Frey is a biochemist who is both a researcher at Health Partners St. Paul-Ramsey Medical Center and a professor at the University of Minnesota. For much of his career, he has been fascinated by a question few other scientists have asked: Why do we cry?

"I wanted to understand how humans alleviate stress," he says in the article "Go Ahead, Cry" by Michael Ryan. Frey found, "The only physiological mechanism we've evolved to [alleviate stress] that is different from every other animal is the ability to cry emotional tears."[9]

Ryan reports that Frey discovered that 85 percent of women and 73 percent of men felt better after they had shed tears in a stressful situation. People are less angry and less sad after crying, Frey found, because tears carry to the brain a unique combination of stress-relieving chemicals at a level thirty times higher than the blood contains: endorphins (painkilling hormones produced after physical exercise) and prolactin (a hormone that helps nursing mothers produce milk).

So, go ahead and cry your eyes out. Wail your gut-splintering rage to the heavens. Know that the Holy Spirit grieves along with you, even for you, in groans which cannot be uttered, according to the will of God (Rom. 8:26-27). Scripture is full of talk about tears. Jesus wept when a friend died (John 11:35). God Himself cries and weeps (Jer. 9:1). In the new heaven, God will wipe away every tear (Rev. 21:4). Jesus was not embarrassed or offended by the woman who washed his feet with her tears (Luke 7:38). He honors and even "bottles" our precious tears (Ps. 56:8).

Where there's pain, there's still feeling. When there's feeling, there's hope. Shed bucketsful! A time is coming "to laugh…to dance…for gathering stones…to hug…to find…to repair…to speak up…for loving…" (Ecc. 3:4-8, TLB). You will be a different person. You will be forever changed by your willingness to confront and embrace your pain.

Sometimes even music cannot substitute for tears.

∼ Paul Simon

The Darker Side of Feelings

Truth. Goodness. Love. We use these words lightly but know so little about them. We're afraid to think or talk about their counterparts. Yet residing within each of us redeemed by Jesus is both the good and the evil of our humanity. Divorce brings to the surface what we have trouble admitting even to ourselves. Another authentic element of feeling-to-heal is encountering the horror of the bad and ugly in ourselves.

K : I remember the day I no longer loved Ed. One Friday afternoon, he came to pick up Melanie at the house I'd just moved into. It was two months before our divorce was final. As he stood on the porch, I thought back to the day I promised to love Ed for a lifetime, my vision clear-cut and defined. Now my eyes traced his face, and I wondered what I had seen in him. How could I have slept with him? What had I trusted? Why? Truth blew me away as the harsh December wind ripped off the roof of my garden shed.

I stared past the facade of the man I had loved into the face of my betrayer. The man who was once my husband was now a stranger. I hardly recognized this person who knew me well enough to wound me. Because I had given him intimate access, he knew the buttons to push to confuse and humiliate me. On the front porch that day, I felt naked.

Isn't that how Adam and Eve saw each other after they feasted on the forbidden fruit? Stripped of innocence. Seeing good and evil. Tasting death.

I closed the door and lingered behind the window curtain. As if in a theater watching a movie about somebody else's life, I watched Ed and his girlfriend drive away with our daughter. Later, my pencil stabbed the word *hate* into a page of my journal. I knew I was looking back at Eden. I had been disrobed. My rose-colored glasses had been ripped away. That day I stared into my own potential for darkness.

> *Man is the only animal that laughs and cries because*
> *he is the only one that can see the difference between*
> *the way things are and the way they ought to be.*
>
> ~ William Hazlitt

N: One evening I sat in front of a fire, surrounded by my children and a couple of their friends. We were watching an inspiring video and in that brief respite, I was savoring hope.

During the climax of the movie, Dan walked through the door without knocking, right in front of the TV, and into my bedroom. I stared, aghast. Just as quickly, he left. Minutes later I found an envelope lying on my pillow addressed with the nickname he used to call me. Surprised, I thought it might contain some positive sentiment.

How wrong I was! I quickly skimmed through a detailed list of my shortcomings. The words and insults of the man before whom I'd bared body and soul jabbed viciously at my femininity. This was the only man I'd ever slept with. I bore his children. He'd promised to cherish and honor me. I was horrified at his cruelty, apparently calculated to hit me just before sleep.

Though it was midnight, I made up my mind. I would find a gun—somewhere, anywhere—take it to his apartment and be done with him.

The problem was, I didn't know where to get a gun. I called a friend instead, livid with murderous thoughts. She kept talking until I was calmer. Then one of my daughters came in and sat beside me on the bed. Her childlike ability to see plainly was like a balm to my spirit. She said with no malice whatever, "Mommy, it's like the devil entered into Daddy and is speaking through him." But I had seen something even more threatening—the evil in me.

The next day, Dan called to apologize for the note. But I felt knocked down and thrown off guard again. Later I was able to discern the pattern he typically used to disarm me by blame or shame, then appeal to my sensitivity or spirituality. Feeling jerked around, my hurt was evolving into hate.

> ***Sometimes, there just aren't enough rocks.***
>
> ∽ Winston Groom, *Forest Gump*

Calling It What It Is

"Evil is real," says M. Scott Peck in *The Road Less Traveled*. "It is not the figment of the imagination of a primitive religious mind feebly attempting to explain the unknown." Peck writes that those who respond to goodness with evil do so without ". . . conscious malice but blindly, lacking awareness of their own evil, indeed seeking to avoid any such awareness. [They]…hate the light because it reveals themselves to themselves. They will destroy the light, the goodness, the love in order to avoid the pain of such self awareness."[10]

Peck defines evil not as *nonlove* (ordinary laziness) but as *antilove*.

Divorce's worst-case scenarios are not just "we don't love each other anymore," or a case of incompatibility—the lazy nonlove Peck refers to. In worst case scenarios there is a profoundly deceptive element functioning under a facade of "goodness." Deceivers deny real feelings (love or hate) and refuse to validate the feelings of others. They can't. The act of feeling, reflecting, or examining the consequences of one's feelings, words, or deeds is too threatening.

But that is exactly what people of integrity have to do. There is no alternative but to turn the tables upside down just as Jesus did in the temple. Do the opposite of what the deceiver expects, what he will not do for himself. Accept the consequences of self-aware-ness—your sin, your own capacity for antilove. Confess it. Grieve it. Ask God's forgiveness. Only such a bold step of holding tightly to the truth breaks the destructive power of evil.

If a thing is free to be good, it is also free to be bad....
Because free will, though it makes evil possible,
is also the only thing that makes possible
any love or goodness or joy worth having.

∽ C.S. Lewis

Good Grief

You are an average woman. You married an ordinary man. You didn't expect wealth, fame, or luxury. You just wanted to love, be loved, and raise a family with a husband in mutual support, faith, and fidelity. You longed for emotional intimacy in marriage. Like us, you are not perfect. You make mistakes. Perhaps he used your imperfection to justify his leaving.

Now you are examining the good, the bad, and the truth about the man you loved. And about yourself. The truth is that a part of you still loves him. In a deep place beyond tears, you cry some days—but not just mourning what you've lost. Though you grieve that your love, sensuality, and best years were spent with an unworthy man, you mourn his loss, too. You wonder if he'll ever face the truth and make the choice to open his own wounds to healing, to feel his feelings, or to talk to somebody.

Grief is about coming to terms with what could have been (a good marriage) while thrusting your fist at what is (divorce).

Your loss includes both the bad and good parts of the marriage. To grieve is to go back and take inventory of what is gone and what remains. Grief immobilizes you. It acts like the lead drape thrown across your body at the dentist's office. It is God's way of slowing you down when your soul has work to do. *Gravare* is Latin for "to burden," and *gravis* means "heavy." Jesus said, "Come to Me, all you who labor and are heavy laden . . ." (Matt. 11:28).

"God's solution for resolving your loss of relationships, dreams, ideals and opportunities is sadness," says Dr. John Townsend. "Rather than something to be avoided, this sadness, or grief, allows you to let go of what you cannot have in order to make room in your heart for what you can have."[11] Sadness does a job.

> *One of the sadder aspects of a good marriage*
> *gone bad is that there are so many pleasant memories*
> *to go with the nightmares.*
>
> ∼ Barbara Cochran Berry

K. Divorce didn't shut me down. It got my attention. For too long my feelings had been invalidated by Ed and denied by me. As I look back on those last two years we were together, I realize I was knitting away at what was already unraveling. A friend observed that toward the end I was more in love with the marriage than the man. I wish you could read my journal entries about the weekends Ed and I spent at our cabin. I labeled it "Our Family's Journey to Sanctuary," but only the brief, final entry, documenting our last Thanksgiving together, says anything real: "November 27. *My heart is heavy.*"

> *Not everything that is faced can be changed,*
> *but nothing can be changed until it is faced.*
>
> ∼ James Baldwin

Hope's Wake-up Call

Grieving can begin in your spirit even before you know what you are grieving about. You can be numbed by a mate's lack of response to love even before you suspect unfaithfulness. The numbness is sometimes simply defined in psychological jargon as "denial," but the issue is really complex, spiritually speaking. Striving to think no evil, bear and believe all things, hope and endure all things (1 Cor. 13:5-7), you tuck the issue to bed. You hope "against hope" that things will get better. But even hope meets its match when it encounters truth. "Hope deferred makes the heart sick," says Proverbs 13:12. The only appropriate response is grief when hope is continuously delayed or denied.

Divorce yanks you out of that bewildering blur. You move from *I can't believe this is happening to me!* to *There must be one more thing I can do to make this work!* Later, you rail, *After all I did for him!* then sink into *What's the use anymore?* At last comes the beautiful sigh, *I think I'm going to make it; maybe life can be even better than before.*

New You Resolution:

Today I determine to face reality. I am going to live this moment.

It is possible to create
light and sound and order within,
no matter what calamity may befall us
in the outer world.

⌒ Helen Keller

One Day Your Downside Will Be Up Again

Be patient with yourself. Listen to your heart and honor it. The writer of Proverbs compared the heart to a reflection that reveals the person you are when no one is looking (Prov. 27:19). Let God take His time healing you. Expect delays and detours. Stop beating yourself up because you can't avoid roadblocks or potholes on the way through divorce.

Always remember how far the Lord has brought you and that your journey is not over yet. You'll never forget the pain; but someday you'll say, "I'm a better person because of what I've gone through. My heart is more tender. My interior life, richer."

Jacque Klippenes, a professional counselor in Castro Valley, California, says, "The key is to understand that God designed us with a tremendous capacity for transparency and vulnerability to live in a world that was innocent. He didn't design us to experience the psychic trauma that may have happened, that kind of hurt. Sin is a phenomenal assault on the mind and heart."

"This is the pay dirt reality," adds Jacque's husband, Jeff, also a counselor. "But into that reality, Christ comes, saying 'I will walk with you guys as flesh. I will feel what you feel, and I think I can help you make sense out of this.' Then it becomes more of a *Columbo* mystery where we begin to play the role of sleuth. We start dogging God, saying, 'Okay, You love me, speak to me about this puzzle. How am I to get empowerment out of this?'"

Jacque urges counseling clients to appreciate the full spectrum of emotion in a divorce: "We get our most reflective understanding when we're hurting, depressed, broken, sad, or angry. At these times, the human soul is most open and available to God."

"Yes," says Jeff, "when God is allowed access to our pain, when we allow the Holy Spirit to energize us, we move forward one step at a time."[12]

The darkest hour is only sixty minutes.

~ Author Unknown

Heart Work:

Great achievers often suffer greatly. Ask yourself:

How might I make the world richer because I've gone through this present distress?

What am I learning about myself?

Three qualities I like about myself are:

> *Though nothing can bring back the hour*
> *Of splendor in the grass,*
> *Of glory in the flower;*
> *We will grieve not, rather find*
> *Strength in what remains behind;*
> *In the primal sympathy*
> *Which having been must ever be;*
> *In the soothing thoughts that spring*
> *Out of human suffering...*

~ William Wordsworth

7

I Am Giving Myself A Chance

*He who dwells in the shelter of the Most High
will rest in the shadow of the Almighty.*

∼ Psalm 91:1, NIV

"*A*ll girls are princesses," Sara told the boarding-school principal. "No matter how poor or ragged or alone; all girls are princesses—didn't *your* father ever tell you that?"

In one moving scene of the film version of Frances Hodgson Burnett's *A Little Princess*, Sara is told her father is dead, and that she is destitute and unwanted. She is taken from her own birthday party, dressed in rags, and led to the dark attic.

Alone, in shock, uprooted from everything she knew to be true and beautiful, Sara slips to the dirty, damp floor. Spying a piece of chalk, she draws a circle around herself and curls up inside it, weeping, "Papa! Papa! Papa!..." She wants to believe the circle is her safe place, within which no evil can penetrate.

A real circle of protection is often mentioned in God's Word; the shadow of His wings (Ps. 17:8), our refuge and fortress (Ps. 91:2), the secret places of the cliff (Song 2:14), a strong tower (Prov. 18:10), our hiding place (Ps. 119:114).

At times, our Heavenly Father becomes the God who hides Himself (Isa. 45:15). In times of loss, fear and despair, we find our way to this circle that contains our broken dreams. It is a safe place. A place to grieve and reflect.

God says, "I will give you the treasures of darkness and hidden riches of secret places..." (Isa. 45:3). All girls are princesses. Like Sara, we too are motivated by what our Father told us. We recognize our calling in spite of evidence to the contrary. We move to bless the world by living out that calling based not on circumstances, but on who we know ourselves to be.

> *Courage doesn't always roar.*
> *Sometimes courage is the quiet voice*
> *at the end of the day saying,*
> *"I will try again tomorrow."*
>
>   ∼ M.A. Hershey

The Safe Place and Beyond

Divorce isolates. Like the little princess, you feel cut off from the familiar, engulfed in circumstances you can't control. You can't imagine the shadow encircling you is a safe place. To dwell in shelter means you rest in shadow. You can't believe you'll ever regroup and step beyond it. But you will.

N: My former position as editor of a national women's magazine was a ringside seat to women's pain. Thousands of letters, manuscripts, and testimonies convinced me that the traditional mode of relating to each other in the church is sadly ineffectual. Human hurt is holy, not something to be hidden away behind a Sunday mask.

The magazine initiated a page of letters, promising readers their personal stories would be listened to and their pain honored, not patronized. Each issue my task included reading dozens of letters and selecting the few to print. I often leaned over my desk, tears dripping onto hand-penned lines. Without conscious knowing, I was within this circle of women, grieving for what was yet to happen to me.

At a writers' conference, I spoke about breaking through artificial spiritual taboos with discretion. Urging writers to go beyond conventional boundaries, I argued for transparency and vulnerability.

A year later, my own courage was tested: I was scheduled to teach again, and no one knew of my divorce. Would I admit the truth, trusting my pain would now be embraced as holy? I decided not to maintain professional distance behind my editor's facade.

One writer, taking courage from my talk the previous year, brought an article proposal on her divorce. I listened, intending to offer rewriting tips. As she elaborated on her manuscript, finally, my emotions collapsed. "Kari," I said, stopping her. "I'm going through this same kind of thing right now." I looked into her bright eyes. "But I want to be like you. I want the twinkle back."

From that moment, we spoke as sisters in Christ. Kari's life affirmed my desire to survive and heal. Her story was published, followed by appreciative letters from other thankful readers. That is how this book was born. By drawing me and others into her circle of experience, she became a safe place, validating my pain and encouraging the move beyond it.

The steadfast love of the Lord never ceases.
His mercies never come to an end.
They are new every morning.

~ Lamentations 3:23, NCV

K ● After Ed moved out, I sensed an invisible shield encircling me about an arm's length from my body. I felt protected within its circumference, although each day brought further confirmation of Ed's affairs. I picked up the sword of the Spirit before bedtime, circling Scripture verses and jotting thoughts in the margins. "Direct my steps by Your word," I prayed with the psalmist, "And let no iniquity have dominion over me" (Ps. 119:133).

One day my fingers froze on the job. My mind flooded with graphic images of Ed with another woman. Then I remembered:

"Thou wilt keep him in perfect peace, whose mind is stayed on thee" (Isa. 26:3, KJV), a verse I'd memorized as a child. My mind cleared. The sword had severed the images.

From that day on, whenever I needed my thoughts cleared, I repeated that verse, at first in its entirety. Eventually, "Thou wilt" was sufficient to allow me to get on with my job. In the middle of the night, when I couldn't silence my pounding chest or still the tapes spinning in my brain, I knelt beside my bed and used the sword to banish demons.

Here, within this place of safety, I discovered the process I now call turnabout thinking.

He is a shield to those who walk in integrity.

∼ Proverbs 2:7, NASB

Turnabout Thinking

Divorce's most brutal battles are fought in the mind. They are about what is true and what is not. Turnabout thinking clarifies what can't be changed and what can. It discriminates between fact and fiction. When your worth is attacked or belief system assaulted, how you define what happens to you determines whether you see opportunities or obstacles, challenges or catastrophes.

Eugene Peterson paraphrased a portion of Paul's letter to the Ephesians (1:18-19) like this: "It is in Christ that we find out who we are and what we are living for. Long before we first heard of Christ and got our hopes up, he had his eye on us, had designs on us for glorious living, part of the overall purpose he is working out in everything and everyone."[1]

The apostle Paul said, "We have the mind of Christ" (1 Cor. 2:16). Becoming empowered through the mind of Christ is what turnabout thinking is all about. It is choosing to think in terms congruent with what God's designs on you are all about and with

His plan for glorious living.

> *Everything can be taken from us but one thing—*
> *the last of the human freedoms—*
> *to choose one's attitude in any given circumstance.*
>
> ～ Victor Frankl

Ask: What Do I Want? What Do I Need?

K. What you want and/or need are not the same thing. Only you know the difference. At least, that's what Melanie's godmother told me when she handed me a legal-sized yellow tablet and said, "Go to it." Thanks to her, I put pen to paper.

I headed for my wants and listed several intangibles like "respect" and other answers listed below. When I looked at the need list, I figured, *Okay, basic survival.* Finally, I realized I could live without my wants but not without my needs. My wants comprise contributions to my life, needs affect who I am at the core of my being, such as hope, peace, and what is eternal. Soon I was on a roll. You will be, too. Go to it!

Wants and Needs

Make two lists side by side. One list may be longer than the other. Write everything you can think of that you want and you need right now.

What I Want—Sample Answers
- Encouragement
- Respect
- Honesty
- Empathy
- Give-and-take in relationships
- Freedom to fail and still be accepted
- Moments when I can be weak
- To know how it feels to have someone else there for me

What I Need—Sample Answers
- Shelter
- Food
- Clothing
- Belonging to a family unit
- Spiritual strength
- Hope for tomorrow
- Peace in my heart and soul
- Time for conversation, reading, exercise, humor

Kari West

A joyful heart makes a cheerful face.…
Bright eyes gladden the heart.

~ Proverbs 15:13, 30, NASB

Define Fact Versus Fiction

Physicians claim optimistic people are less susceptible to depression and illness.[2] They say feelings of helplessness and/or hopelessness cause the brain to manufacture hormones that weaken the immune system. Before any studies were published, the writer of Proverbs said, "The spirit of a man will sustain him in sickness, But who can bear a broken spirit?" (Prov. 18:14).

A way to stay optimistic and gain back control of your emotions is to distinguish between fact and fiction in your divorce. See the truth in black and white. For example, if you are agonizing over your children enjoying fun-filled weekends with the other parent while labeling you the "do-your-homework-feed-the-cat-empty-the-trash mom," this exercise will help clarify your responsibilities and maximize your objectivity.

Facts or Fiction

Write side-by-side lists: Facts About My Marriage, Fiction About My Marriage. Do the same about your children and about your ex. Define and hold on to what is good. Discover it was not all bad.

Facts About My Marriage—Sample Answers
• Seventeen years were good; I still have those memories
• I enjoyed the cabin for two-and-a-half years
• I did too much
• Divorce could be a new beginning

Fiction About My Marriage—Sample Answers
• All twenty-two years were bad
• The cabin was a mistake
• I could have done more to save my marriage
• My life is completely ruined

Facts About My Children—Sample Answers
• I am doing whatever I can for my daughter
• In joint custody she'll observe inconsistencies in both lifestyles
• Our relationship is strained
• By giving her up to God, I lessen her dad's control of me through her

Fiction About My Children—Sample Answers
• I am the only one who can help my daughter
• It's all her dad's fault
• Changes that I make to please her will help our relationship
• I could have done more to make things better

Facts About My Ex—Sample Answers
• He lies and manipulates
• He is jealous of how I kept my life in order
• He has committed adultery multiple times

Fiction About My Ex—Sample Answers
• Appealing to his conscience gets me somewhere
• Being depressed over him is worth the effort
• Mentally rewriting the past into perfect scenes helps me

Kari West

Any man can fight the battle for just one day.
It is only when you and I add
the burden of those two awful eternities,
yesterday and tomorrow, that we tremble.

~ John Maxwell

Redefinition

Divorce forces you to release many ideals in search of what is real. You look long and hard for bedrock values and a new direction because you desperately want to live and move on. You begin to understand the most important word about going through divorce is the word *through*. It carries you like a raft over the current of tormented thoughts and grief threatening to over-whelm. Other times, you traverse rough terrain on foot. Six mile-stones identify your passage as you make choices that redefine dreams and circumstances.

1: *Own What Is Real*
At some point you finally decide *if there is an experience in front of me, I will own it.* Although you hate the scar this crisis will leave, the good thing is you are addressing—or dressing—the wound. You are not denying or running from it. You stare your greatest fear in the face and acknowledge, *Yes, this is really happening to me.*
From that moment on, you move forward.

N: Trying to resolve what I didn't understand, I turned over my questions like puzzle pieces. *Had I done something terrible to deserve this? Why hadn't my faith helped save our marriage? How could the Heavenly Father I'd believed since childhood have let me go on trusting Dan? How could I bear the failure of a broken family* and divorce? Could I ever believe again that all things work together for good to those who love God?

I had to admit I was a participant in allowing the space between Dan and me to grow. I kept tolerating his move away from emotional and physical intimacy, hoping and believing that giving the gift of space and trust would turn things around. I had accepted too little, overlooked too much, and carried buckets much too small to the well of prayer. Finally, I realized faith allows mercy to do its job, but faith can't control other people's choices. God, in His mercy, gave Dan year after year until God said, "Enough is enough."

I read about Gerald Sittser, who lost his wife, mother, and daughter in an automobile accident and said, "I absorbed the loss into my life like soil receives decaying matter until it became a part of who I am."[3] As he was, I'm fertilized by the experience. I am enduring with dignity. I look people in the eye and am proud of my daughters who have bravely borne their share.

When I examine dreams available to me, it's clear I most want what I always did: to be the wife of a godly man and serve God together with my family. Each day I choose to believe God is still on the job, working on what I can't see.

2. Let Go of What Isn't

Some of what you always believed just isn't true. Like a fog lifting, illusions vaporize. You feel confused, and you rage against the injustice of it all. You are in a battle to let go of a person and a way of life. You give it up and just as quickly take it back.

Take courage, because change is tough. There are rude aftershocks. You may be surprised at your own blackness of heart. You feel like you'll always feel this way. But you won't. Somewhere along that seemingly never-ending road labeled *YOU'LL NEVER FIGURE THINGS OUT,* you see a marker pointing onward. You tell yourself, *I won't always be in this place.* You're starting to let go.

K: As soon as I moved into my own house, my friend Barney, who is a child evangelist, challenged me to give beyond my normal tithe. I thought, *He doesn't understand my financial situation.* As an independent contractor, my income depended on job availability. "Okay, thirty-five dollars," I blurted out, figuring to myself, *What's that on top of my other losses?* In reality, Barney's challenge was about releasing fear's grip on my mind, freeing me for impossibilities: surviving a twenty-five-dollar checkbook balance. Restoration of my relationship with Melanie. Trusting again. Remarriage.

3. Challenge the Status Quo

You're looking through new eyes now beyond the old landscape. At first, you avoid things that make you feel bad—the bakery that made your wedding cake, the teller at the bank. You change bakeries and banks, though they're blocks out of your way.

What things make you feel good? You light candles for ambience, take bubble baths instead of showers, ask a friend to call you every day. When you examine the myths in your life, you see they can be changed. For example, at first you believe it is good to vent your rage in outbursts. As you indulge, you see that merely pumps up the brain's arousal system. You find other ways to deal with anger: distraction, exercise, reforming the situation in a positive light. You can't change things, so you decide to change the way you think about them.

You are creating a context of success for yourself.

N: When I read Isaiah 54, I stopped at verse 2: "Enlarge the place of your tent."

I took it literally and began to cultivate my lawn to the property line. Then I took it spiritually and acknowledged that my marriage partner betrayed himself each time he operated out of lust instead of love. And I made the most important decision of all: to affirm each evening that something larger would come out of my crisis.

Keep looking up…
That's where God likes to put the rainbows.

~ Author Unknown

4. Open Your Heart

You know now you will not die, though you may have wished you would. You think the world may eventually become safe again. You recognize the adventure of going to a place you've never been requires a contribution from you.

Now you focus on the woman before the wound. You wonder how to meet her again. To imagine and wonder is part of your work right now. Soon there is an intersection: one path leading to the past, the other straight ahead and up a hill. Mountains loom behind the hill, but there is no question in your mind anymore.

You put your heart into the journey.

K. After we'd agreed to separate, but before Ed moved out, my divorced friend Eleanor offered her house as a safe place. She gave me a front-door key and cleared floor space in her hall closet where I could leave private papers. Many mornings, after dropping Melanie at school and before driving to work, I retreated to the privacy of Eleanor's living room. I needed this safe place to collect my thoughts.

But Eleanor did more than create a safe place for me. She inspired me to create safe places for myself. I splurged on a fancy bath towel with a lace-ruffled border and on a coffeemaker with a programmable timer for hazelnut-scented wake-up calls. Much later, I envisioned the possibility of sitting across the table from a wonderful man who sipped coffee from a matching mug. It was then that I knew: if I ever remarried, he had to love coffee (and he does!).

More importantly, I observed that Eleanor carried herself with flair. I was drawn to her enthusiasm and admired how she had put her divorce behind her. She was turning her hobby of oil painting into a business and had bought her own home and new dishes, and had changed many things in between. She smiled a lot. "The kind of men who sneak around and walk out on marriages are not worth crying over," she said.

5. *Put One Foot in Front of the Other*

It is simple. You just keep going, though you stumble now and then. You pick a wild flower while you're down. Occasionally there is a boulder in the path. You make a choice: rage at the injustice of it being there, roll it out of the way, or find a detour. You're begging to believe in your ability to make decisions again. You are patient with your mistakes. One day at a time is good enough. That becomes your slogan. Without realizing it, you are marshaling your own feelings of enthusiasm.

With every step, you gain confidence. Your energy becomes self-motivating for all the times you are going to stub your toe. You do what you have to do.

N: At a conference early in my divorce, a young married man sat by me at dinner and said, "I heard what you are going through. How in the world do you get up in the morning?"

I told him, "I have three children who need breakfast and to get off to school—that's how and why I get up."

6. *Don't Look Back*

After all, "You're not going that way," it says in a book illustrated by Mary Engelbreit.[4] However, you won't be able to count the times you'll be tempted to do so. Sometimes you forcibly pull your chin around straight and steady your eyes with a chuckle of self-irony.

Now the possibility of real happiness is on the horizon. You are happy for the depth of character, the insight, the compassion, the change in yourself. You still haven't figured everything out, but you no longer feel you need to. Your circumstances may be imperfect, but good feelings begin to outweigh bad ones. You wear your scars like medals. You are glad you hung in there.

You are reinventing your life.

K: When I telephoned my parents about the possibility of a divorce, Dad said: "After a decision is made, don't look back." At first, I wrestled with Ed's decision to leave; then my own resolution to walk on with or without him. I realized someone must have been working hard to make the marriage last twenty-two years; something worked.

As the years roll on, I realize a broader application. When I'm tempted to compare myself to other divorced women on issues like joint custody and letting go of our home, I don't think, *Hey, I should have done such and such.* I look to what's ahead. Knowing I did my best with what I had at the time, I rise above regret and recrimination.

Spiritually, I now see that in a world gone wrong, it's not that God doesn't make sense. I accept that His children make choices that don't make sense. I can't do anything about that, but I know I'm part of a picture God continues to enlarge. Like Job, I've heard about the Lord all my life (Job 42). Now I'm looking forward. The best is now and may be waiting in all the moments yet to be.

> ***Effective people are not problem-minded;***
> ***they're opportunity-minded.***
> ***They feed opportunities and starve problems.***
>
> ∽ Steven Covey

New You Resolution:

Today I will change the way I think about one thing in my life.

Seeing Further

Now you are ready to look at possibilities your Heavenly Father saw before you were born. When all windows and doors to the future are barricaded, seize this golden moment. Walk to the wall and paint a window. Open it and crawl through it. The art is in knowing which reality is the illusion: the window closed in your face? or the one you paint and through which you pass to start the rest of your life?

"All girls are princesses," Sara said as she imagined warm muffins and soft, woolly blankets in her bare attic room, not knowing in the morning it would come true. Perhaps Frances Hodgson Burnett, author of *A Little Princess*, had been reading Isaiah 54:11, 12, 14: "O you afflicted one, Tossed with tempest and not comforted, Behold I will lay your stones with colorful gems and lay your foundations with sapphires. I will make your pinnacles of rubies, Your gates of crystal....In righteousness you shall be established; You shall be far from oppression...."

The psalmist wrote, "O Lord, you have searched me and known me" (Ps. 139:1). *Chaqar,* the Hebrew word for "searched," is a mining term. It means to probe or examine and carries the connotation of God digging through you deeply, as for jewels. You are of great worth.

Didn't your Heavenly Father ever teach you that?

P.S. We love you!

Heart Work:

What can I do today to become the person I want to be tomorrow?

8

I Am Not
Disappearing

How precious to me are your thoughts, O God!
How vast is the sum of them!
Were I to count them,
they would outnumber the grains of sand.

∼ Psalm 139:17-18, NIV

$\mathcal{K}$: "I like what we are becoming," Richard said. My husband's shoulder nudged mine as we strolled along the Pacific shoreline recently. Several steps ahead, Melanie and the dogs skipped through salty surf. We had come here for lots of reasons—to soak up sunshine on this windy Thanksgiving; to let go of past memories and to make new ones.

I stuck my bare feet into the sand, digging toes into scattered clumps of broken shells. Crouching, I combed the grains for one single whole shell, but found none. A jogger whizzed by. I stood up and glanced at the trail of footprints and paw prints. In that moment I understood a truth that had eluded me before.

The Creator sees my life not as odd pieces, scattered clumps, or crushed parts of what once was whole, but as a wide, wonderful beach engraved with His own footprints. My worth is not defined by success or failure, joy or sorrow, marriage or divorce. These are just part of the picture. Divorce, by forcing me to the end of myself, was opening me to a world of possibilities much larger than myself.

That day I realized my brokenness was touching many lives with love, hope, and purpose. Finally, I saw my journey as ongoing. Life's losses are never wasted particles but an immeasurable part of who I am becoming.

Why else were individuals created, but that God, loving all infinitely, should love each differently.

~ C.S. Lewis

N: One weekend I borrowed a friend's beach condo. It was stormy on the Oregon coast. One or two people braved the weather, leaving footprints in the wet sand. Most stayed behind picture windows watching clouds move swiftly across the sky. Dressed in a hooded windbreaker, I headed north, dodging waves breaking into foam at my feet.

The beach was desolate—like my mood. Clean swept by waves. Whipped by blustering winds. Bleak. By the time I reached the curve in the shoreline, I was soaking wet. I faced into the pelting rain, hard after something I was unable to define, then came upon a sunken hollow in the sand about six feet wide. Every available sea shell seemed to have been swept here—thousands, now crushed among pebbles and stones in the pounding surf.

I stepped into the hollow, my spirit like lead. *This is me, Lord,* I said. *Crushed. Broken. Trampled.*

Then I saw it lying radiant as light against the gray-brown backdrop. Perfectly whole. Perfectly white. A three-inch shell, God's object lesson on a vacant stretch of coastline. Promise of wholeness, purity, and what was to be. I carried it home, touched by the impossibility of its being there at all.

What You Are Becoming

Perhaps you, too, have meditated to the familiar music of wind and waves and pounding surf. You prayed and carried away a meaning that is uniquely yours. As it should be. Whether you see yourself as part of a beach or a whole shell, the truth is that your worth is infinite.

"In math, if you divide an infinite number by any number, no matter how large, you still have an infinite quotient," said Charles Spurgeon, history's most widely read preacher. "So Jesus' love, being infinite, even though it is divided up for every person on earth, is still infinitely poured out on each one of us!"[1]

When your trembling toes sink deep into life's cold surf and fog engulfs you, you are not disappearing. When you think your troubles "are heavier than the sand of a thousand seashores" (Job 6:3, TLB), you are not disappearing. You are becoming. Your losses are becoming a wide, wonderful beach.

K. After filing for divorce, Ed procrastinated two months before moving out. Melanie stayed with him that first weekend after he moved. I awoke early Sunday morning and spent a couple hours paying bills before church. When I returned, the empty house felt like a tomb. I was so down I telephoned our associate pastor and his wife who lived two doors away, Rod and Dot Towes. They invited me over. I could be vulnerable with them. Both had experienced an unwanted divorce. Their advice felt credible.

"Regardless of what happened, dare to dream," Rod told me. "Live with vision of what your life will be three months, six months, a year, five years from now. Have a vision for every area of your life—your job, where you'll live, new friends—what God's plan might be for the rest of your life."

Dot pulled her chair closer and looked into my eyes. "And don't overlook the fact that God is concerned with your personal life," she said. "If it's your heart's desire, have a vision of the Lord bringing into your life someday a godly husband, who will love and care for you more than you've ever been loved or cared for before—a man who will be there for you in all integrity and fidelity."

Even before I imagined a future, God was already affirming there was one. I determined to dare to dream, the way Rod suggested. I had no idea that in the morning my heart was to be further crushed. Melanie's conversation with "the cleaning lady" brought Ed's affairs to the surface. I felt like Job: "He breaks me down on every side, and I am gone" (Job 19:10). Later that night I scribbled through my tears: "Thank you, Lord, that I can think of this as a turning point. As Rod said, give me vision. I officially mentally end my relationship with Ed. Emotionally, help me end it, too."

With hindsight, I realize that mental determination and emotional strength was not what got me through the days that followed. What helped most was learning to live with vision. I clung to an eternal hope of seeing God (Job 19:25). But I also needed a get-through-the-day hope, like the simple faith of a child sitting on heavenly shoulders, reaching beyond circumstances, touching stars. I wanted to believe God was ordering my jobs at work and that a good man out there was looking for a woman just like me. The days I could pull this off made me feel different. Rod and Dot helped me combine a hopeful attitude (faith) with a mental picture (vision).

The next step was behaving as if I believed it.

> *But forget all that—*
> *it is nothing compared to what I'm going to do!*
> *For I'm going to do a brand new thing.*
> *See, I have already begun!*
> *Don't you see it?*
>
> ～ Isaiah 43:18, 19, TLB

How Your Negatives Are Developing into Positives

It takes a courageous kind of vision…

- to pop open a new calendar, thumb through months of pretty pictures, and wonder what's ahead.

- to imagine the secrets your DayTimer will reveal by year's end.

- to believe you'll survive the turmoil of sending your kids to their dad for summer vacation.

- to imagine Mr. Wonderful is still out there after months of dead-end dates and lonely weekends.

Along with embracing truth, vision is another part of the hard work of healing. It is not sponge-cake faith but holy terror—shaking and believing anyway. Vision is not passive wait-and-see. It is acting as if you believe, though there are no visible or immediate results. Like letting go and forgiveness, it is a get-moving-and-watch-what-happens mentality.

Vision: you either "get it" and move on or you remain behind. You invest in your dream or declare bankruptcy. You figure there is nothing more to lose, so you do for yourself what you can do because God has a big investment in you. You are beach-front property.

Visionary people are excited, encouraged, enthusiastic. When they feel fatigued, God cooperates with their humanity. When they reach what seems like the end of the road, little miracles happen to prod them on their way again.

Elijah ran for his life from Jezebel into the wilderness, praying for death under a broom tree (I Kings 19:1-8). God's angel did a very human thing: touched him and baked him a cake. Elijah went out in the strength of that miracle forty days and nights; God gave him a new commission.

Pregnant Hagar ran from Sarai into the wilderness. An angel found her by a spring and made her a promise which restored her vision for the child within her and gave her the will to live. Hagar called the name of the Lord *You-Are-the-God-Who-Sees* (Gen. 16:6-13).

Living with vision is a daring adventure. It is wild abandonment, releasing, holding everything loosely—including the rest of your life. It is not focusing on specific results but on a quality life in the present moment. It is daring yourself to behave as if you believe something is going to happen; putting yourself into a position that makes it possible to happen.

Imagination is the highest kite that one can fly.

∼ Lauren Bacall

N: The beach was crowded: kids, dogs, lovers, sunbathers, sand-castle builders, and kite flyers tugging at cords that held whirling rainbows in all shapes and sizes. I had hoped to get absorbed in the fun but was wrestling pain again—like Jacob wrestling with the angel. *I-will-not-let-you-go-unless-you-bless-me* kind of wrestling: prolonged, lonely, wearying. Determined.

Is there anything in my future for which it is worth hanging on tight? I wondered, remembering that four years earlier Dan and I celebrated our sixteenth wedding anniversary on a nearby beach. In the sand, he'd written I LOVE YOU, circled by a giant heart. Together, we'd conceived a ministry dream.

Eventually, the dream eroded like Dan's love message in the sand, pummeled by waves and the trails of passers-by. With Dan gone, I realized the vision was as counterfeit as his wedding vows. Wrestling with the angel that day on the beach, I heard: *This is the sacrifice. Like broken water in childbirth, your broken heart, flooding your life with tears, will usher in an authentic dream.*

Though I was certain I did not want to live this vision on my own, all I could say on the beach that day was, *Lord, here I am.*

Write injuries in the sand, kindnesses in marble.

∼ French Proverb

How Are We Then to Live?

"It all began with a wrong turn," writes Jack Hayford. "But for the grace of God, the story could have ended in tragedy, bitterness and death. God had something else in mind. And because He did, we have one of the most beautiful love stories ever told."[2]

Hayford elaborates on the story of Ruth, a woman of vision. He says that her husband, in moving from Israel to Moab was looking for a new time and place, yet on his own terms. He was a man under duress seeking an answer outside the boundaries of God's provision for His people, looking for life in all the wrong places.

"Outside the boundaries of the covenant," Hayford says, "You and I will ultimately find what Elimelech, Mahlon and Chilion found—death. The untimely passing of these men is not an act of an angry God smashing a little family into the asphalt of Moab's streets. It is simply a commentary on what happens outside the covenant....Elimelech is a man who chased a rainbow and lost an inheritance. He took his family with him and they lost everything too—including him."[3]

Hayford continues, "Before the lost could be redeemed, someone needed to retrace that costly journey and return to the place of blessing."

Retracing the journey takes vision. "Not knowing what hardships or heartaches lay ahead of her in a foreign land," Hayford concludes, "Ruth chose to cling to what was left of her new family rather than returning to the old. In so doing, she placed herself in a position to find a new time and place. The Bible says she *clung* to Naomi. She wasn't about to be turned away."[4]

Now that's vision. Ruth placed herself in a position, within the boundaries of the covenant, to find her purpose and meaning. She was unwilling to be turned away. Vision empowers because it allows you to see that your worth in this world hinges on a bigger picture—God's love for you. His love gifts you with a reality worth waiting for and hanging onto tightly.

Vision isn't about a health-wealth-happiness gospel or about channeling, psychotherapy, or autogenic training. It is about the conviction that loss equals gain, hurt can equal hope, and pain brings renewed purpose. It is knowing the *God-Who-Sees* and aligning your sight with His. Vision is being confident "that He who has begun a good work in you will complete it" (Phil. 1:6). "Therefore we do not lose heart....The inward man is being renewed day by day" (2 Cor. 4:16).

So how do you start living with vision?

Kick the devil out of your hope chest

Maybe you would like a new relationship or a different job. Perhaps it's time to sell the family home and buy a condo in another town. Or you've been approached to facilitate the church single-again group. But you're afraid. What if somebody rejects you? What if you fail?

Perhaps you know what you want and you go for it. You begin to date again, go for a promotion, or move to a new place. You get hurt. You feel defeated all over again. Maybe you volunteer to teach a class or you decide to throw a Christmas party. You fall in love, then are disappointed and disillusioned. Either way, the devil has inserted the key of fear into your hope chest and hopped in. His plan is to wear you down (Dan. 7:25), crush your spirit, and steal your new dream.

Living with vision, "behaving as if you believe it," kicks the devil out. You see with new eyes. Vision is magnetic and attracts like-minded people. Hope becomes a lifestyle.

Ecclesiastes 11:4-5 says to get on with things regardless of how the wind is blowing, because you never know what God is up to. God might blow something really good your way out of nowhere when you least expect it! Get out there. Give what you've got to give.

Place an order for fish and chips to go

Give Jesus everything in your basket right now—even if you think it doesn't amount to much (Matt. 14:15-20). After He blesses and breaks it, you'll find there's plenty to pass around.

> *One of the greatest sins a Christian can commit …*
> *is the sin of unreached potential.…*
> *We allow our patterns of life to become frozen*
> *and our achievements have such low ceilings*
> *that we allow ourselves the comfort of convenience.*
>
> ∼ Tim Hansel

K • "If there's something you feel God has called you to do and you haven't done it yet, why not?" challenged Dr. Mark Lee at a family church camp.

At the time, I shuddered at the question. My life is more uncertain than ever, I thought. That day at camp, with our ten year old seated between us, Ed and I looked like any other "happy" family; but it was a mirage. In one week, our trial separation would begin.

After high school I had taken a job as a secretary to support myself through night school. Then I married Ed and worked while he got his degrees. Later I earned the family's second income. I had always put my life on hold for him.

But I'd always known I wanted to write. Childhood vacations were spent perched on river banks, scribbling wild and wonderful stories about pictures cut from old catalogs, while my parents fished. My grandmother insisted I tuck poems inside letters to her. Journalism teachers said, "I like the way you write."

What did God expect of me? I wondered that day at camp. I knew only too well why I had not done it, and I saw no way possible in the future. After our seven-month separation, Ed stayed for two years. Then, like the catastrophic 1989 earthquake that opened San Francisco's waterfront view by knocking down a freeway, God allowed my divorce to reveal talents hidden for two decades behind Ed's dream. I began to see clearly and to write about what I saw. I wanted to help other people see things clearly, too.

When I remarried and was freed from the pressure of earning a second income, the stories and articles started to flow and scattered across the pages of numerous magazines. God had prepared me years before, but He was patient. When the time was right, I picked up the vision.

> *I pray that your hearts will be flooded with light*
> *so that you can see something of the future*
> *he has called you to share....*
> *I pray that you will begin to understand*
> *how incredibly great his power is*
> *to help those who believe him.*
>
> ～ Ephesians 1:18-19, TLB

N: The shoreline was misty. I promised myself I wouldn't come here again in fall, but the northwest coast is rarely clear. I drag my body through the piney trees to the beach. To think. Walking through pea soup, I pray. Imagine. Skip. Laugh.

My journey through singleness-again is taking me backwards. All the way back to the five-year-old me, that little girl who wanted to dance ballet. I am reinventing that girl: Independent. Proud of herself for the gifts she is exploring.

The ocean breeze is gentle, like my thoughts about myself. I am enjoying the new freedom of having young-adult children. Although I often find myself wistful for the hectic days of babies, or angry at being abandoned in midlife, good days now outnumber bad ones. I am reclaiming the woman-before-the-wound—way before.

Two people emerge arm-in-arm from the sandy bank behind me. They stop and embrace. Kiss. I hurt again. I want that. The sensual woman, too, is part of who I am. As her husband grew distant and uninterested, she longed for languid nights of intimacy. I still crave what almost every woman does: a man's emotional presence, pursuit, and passion. *I want to love again. Is this an endurance test?* I ask God.

He says, *Pray for the man in the wings.* He says, *Keep becoming the kind of woman the kind of man you want would be attracted to.*

I am vulnerable, strong, weak, feminine, silly, scared, brave all at one time. I date a little. I even fall in love, but grasping at another relationship is as illusive as holding fog. How can a person ever be sure? I keep going; keep thinking about all I have to give and who the lucky man will be. I'm amazed how far I have come!

If you want to leave your footprints
on the sands of time,
be sure you're wearing work boots.

∼ Italian Proverb

Look, It Is Not as You Once Thought

Refuse to be content with myopic vision. Life is too short to stay nearsighted or narrowminded. Pull out your telescope. Stretch your faith. Choose to multiply God's majesty, not magnify your misery.

Vision leads past a poverty mind-set to a generosity mentality. When you see more, you give and receive more. Vision is praying for a larger map. To Joshua was given the promise: "Every place that the sole of your foot will tread upon, I have given you" (Josh. 1:3). God thinks big. He marks territory from one end of a desert to the setting of the sun and back.

"Our ideas about God are so neat and tidy, so symmetrical and right-side-up," writes Joni Eareckson Tada. "We have the Sunday School medals and threadbare Bibles to prove that we've gotten Him pretty much figured out, at least all the important stuff. Not too many things astonish us these days. But when is the last time you were surprised by the Lord?"

"Broaden your vision," Tada says. "Avoid snap judgments about His Word. Focus beyond the expected. Let the Lord keep you in perpetual wonder. I have a feeling that the Lord is less interested in what we know and more interested in helping us look beyond to see the impossible."[5]

Jabez grew up expecting God to work; he had a vision and he went to God with it. He also had baggage; his name was a reminder of how much pain he was to his mother. "Oh, that you would bless me and enlarge my territory!" he prayed. The village bearing his name was the home of scribes (1 Chron. 4:9-10).

Habakkuk clung to the Lord even when his nation didn't and even though things happened he didn't understand (Hab. 3:16-19). He held on to what he couldn't see. His name comes from the verb "to embrace."

Caleb, whose name means "good," was given the land on which he set foot because he and his sons followed the Lord "fully" (Deut. 1:36).

To not follow fully is to lose much. Living with vision requires the whole heart. How often are you a mere footstep away from a promise?

New You Resolution:

Today I will be expectant, on tiptoes. I will look for God's footprints on my beach.

One sees great things from the valley;
only small things from the peak.

~ G.K. Chesterton

Seeing Things as They Are

Living with vision you move from defining yourself as a bore, a blur, or a bum who was in your ex-husband's way, to seeing yourself as God sees you. You're no longer wondering, *What will I do if I run into my ex?* You're now hoping to bump into him so he'll see how great you look. You have quit thinking, *I can't go to the big sale downtown because I might see his girlfriend.* You now imagine her expression when you look her right in the eye. You might even smile, then take yourself out for an amaretto latte! (Go ahead, admit what you're thinking. *The poor thing looks so frumpy! All that wining and dining went straight to her hips!)*

Place your circumstances beneath your feet; don't just wait for them to pass. Stride with your face into the wind, prepared for the wave of the future. ". . . There's no stopping it," says Anne Morrow Lindbergh. Build your sand castle with turrets and towers all over. Dig a moat that's deeper. Decorate with wave-polished stones and shiny shells. Play harder. Run further. Fly a kite. Soar!

You see, with vision you can hardly wait to flip open your calendar. Whatever it holds, you can face it.

The real voyage of discovery
consists not in seeking
new landscapes
but in having new eyes.

∾ Marcel Proust

Heart Work:

What is your vision of what your life will be three months, six months, a year, five years from now? for the rest of your life?

It is never too late to be
what you might have been.

∾ George Eliot

Copy and tuck this poem in your wallet. Read it every day for thirty days.

∾ If I Can Live Believing:

 . . . the most beautiful sunset is coming tomorrow

 . . . the greatest meadow is the one beyond the mountain

 . . . the closest friendship waits to be formed

 . . . the deepest love is still being created

 . . . the best answer to my prayers is already on its way

Then my life will be one of hope, expectation, and joy and I shall be of all people most blessed.

Anonymous

9

It's Okay
To Lighten Up
And Let Go

Cease striving (let go) and know that I am God.

⁓ Psalm 46:10, NASB—The Open Bible Expanded Edition.

K: What person standing beside the ocean's edge has not wondered about the world concealed in mystery beneath its restless surface? I did—and decided to do something about it. I learned to scuba dive. But because I get seasick on boats, I content myself with diving off the beach.

Confined inside a full-length body suit, gloves, and snorkel mask, my five-foot frame slowly trudges along the sandy beach into the rushing tide. I struggle with each step as wet sand sucks against my boots. With each forward motion, I feel the steel air tank dragging on my back, the fourteen-pound lead weight belt slapping my hip bones, and the foot-long instrument console swinging from the left side of my buoyancy-control vest.

The weight I carry feels unbearable as I slosh through the steel-grey swells—until I press the low-pressure air valve to inflate my vest. Soon I bob like a cork. My dangling feet tell me the sandy bottom has dropped off.

I hang for a moment suspended between two worlds. As I float into open ocean, I rinse the mask lens and breathe into the regulator to make sure it's operational. Then I snap on fins, set the depth gauge, and deflate my vest; the weight I had struggled to carry now takes me down.

Below, the sun's rays skip across the edges of a coral reef. I enter a garden of creatures wiggling in unison. Purple anemones wave slender tentacles. Spotted unicorn fish nudge my arm. A white-mouth moray eel pops out of a rocky ledge, and I hyper-ventilate. *Stay calm,* I tell myself.

I add air to stop my descent, equalizing my weight with the water, and achieve neutral buoyancy. The jagged coral can slice my leg if I get too close. Here, I have learned to breathe through my mouth, not my nose, and to continually monitor the air pressure to ensure enough remains for my ascent. The amount of air I use and the depth of my descent determine the length of my dive.

It sounds complicated. But each time I sojourn into this weightless world, the experience is punctuated with mystery. It is ultimate solitude. The only sound I hear is my own exhaling. I can swim in any direction or somersault like a dolphin undulating with the rhythm of the sea. I am free.

> *For our light affliction, which is but for a moment,*
> *is working for us a far more exceeding*
> *and eternal weight of glory.*
>
> ∼ 2 Corinthians 4:17

Taking the Plunge

As in diving, the weight of life's losses in divorce is forcing you to leave the surface and go deeper. If you choose to stay within safe confines under the shelter of wide umbrellas, you will miss the adventure of falling free—abandoning to Him who holds all things together (Col. 1:17). Divorce also teaches you to breathe in a new way and to trust the only life support you need. In your own mysterious under-"see" drama, you are the protagonist coming face-to-face with your antagonist: life. Each time you dive beneath the predictable, you're apprehensive. But you are learning how to face your fears without wasting resources.

At first, your reflex is like a beginning diver drifting over an undersea ledge that suddenly plunges twenty feet. You grab hold so you won't fall. Sudden change, like the elevator effect, catches you unprepared and creates anxiety. The irony is you have achieved buoyancy; you're already floating. Now, instead of clutching people, places, and possessions for your identity and security, you are learning to let go. You fine-tune your weight between faith and doubt, glide over things you used to crash into, maintain equilibrium between too heavyhearted and too light. The more you practice, the more proficient you become.

K. • After Ed left, I kept hearing, *Let go and I will bless you.* At the time, I didn't understand this would be one of the most difficult choices I would make, nor did I know it would be ongoing.

Early on I started releasing my grip. Things that Ed and I possessed together no longer had meaning. Jewelry he'd given me felt tainted as I questioned his motives. I relinquished interest in his business, agreed to joint custody of our daughter, sold furniture, gave clothing to charity.

With Ed gone, I was less distracted emotionally and had more energy to compare my rising suspicions with the paperwork. What I discovered pulled the bottom out from under me; but it was too late. I agonized over the decision to reopen our settlement. I wanted justice! Legal and spiritual counselors advised: Let go. Intuitively, I sensed, *there's more here than I can handle.*

I feared Ed. I was stunned he could use the education I'd helped him get against me. However, fear of losing my health and sanity was greater. What I needed most was peace of mind. Confrontation was pointless. Battling in court might take years and keep me stuck in the past.

"In blind trust," I wrote, "I must emptyhandedly dare to walk toward the future." Letting go was not a helpless resignation but a deliberate turning away from everything familiar to me—only my daily commute on the freeway stayed the same.

A couple of weeks later, Barney appeared at my door to shepherd me with this familiar verse: "...that I may apprehend that for which also I am apprehended of Christ Jesus....This one thing I do, forgetting those things which are behind, and reaching forth unto those things which are before..." (Phil. 3:12-13, KJV). I read it over and over. I experienced everything *apprehend(sive)* conveys: to be fearful and suspicious, to understand, to take into custody, and to forgive. It took every fiber within me to let go: of the past, my angry desire to blast Ed about how he hurt me. Even today, I face revelations and residue from those years. Letting go is how I cope with life's insanity as I take the plunge.

> *What light? I'm still looking for the tunnel!*
>
> ∽ Barbara Johnson

Weighting It Out: The Paradox of Lightening Up

Since life's currents are dragging you out to sea, you might as well go deeper. It may sound confusing but, lightening up is a prerequisite to that. It is active waiting, suspended between bifurcated worlds—the temporal and the eternal. As you prepare for both the descent and ascent, you experience good and evil, joy and sorrow, light and dark, up and down.

"The ladder whose ascent implies spiritual progress has a long pedigree," writes Hillman. "The upward idea of growth has become a biographical cliché. To be an adult is to be a grown-up...[but] until the culture recognizes the legitimacy of growing down, each person in the culture struggles blindly to make sense of the darkenings and despairings that the soul requires to deepen into life."[1]

If you want your heavy experiences to take you deeper, you have to let go of surface expectations—things and emotions that keep you stuck. It is essential to lay aside what holds you back (Heb. 12:1). Letting go and growing down is the only way to have open hands ready to receive the life that is waiting for you. Once in the deep, weight and buoyancy become your allies.

N: Weighted! My philosophy is "you can't be too thin or too rich," but during my three pregnancies, I found that weight gain can mean value-added. I welcomed it, knowing a new possibility was growing inside me. The hard part was waiting to see what would be.

I heard that in Scandanavian languages, the word *expecting* is "to wait." *"Are you pregnant?"* is literally, "Are you waiting?" But these times of waiting were the most active times in my life: childbirth exercises, classes, and reading. There was time spent picking a name and preparing healthier-than-usual food, meals for the freezer, furniture for the baby's room, the layette—all the time belly and breasts getting heavier until I felt like a mythological goddess. Still, I savored every moment, knowing that the day would come when I would lighten up. I knew my "burden" would one day be born, taking on a life of his or her own, full of potential, expressing qualities and abilities of which I could only dream. And so it is with divorce, this new kind of burden.

If there's an experience in front of you, have it!

~ Author Unknown

The Way of Letting Go

Letting go is the ultimate way to say, "Your kingdom come. Your will be done" (Matt. 6:10). Although hard to understand right now, your circumstances are, like Jonah in the belly of the whale, an opportunity in disguise. Your fear is your limit; letting go is not for cowards. It has nothing to do with give up and give in. You move ahead while waiting actively for the mystery to unfold. By letting go of the happy ending to your original dream, you reposition yourself, weighted in reality. You understand more than you ever thought possible.

Letting go of the way things were sets you free. It allows your former spouse the freedom to make choices, accountable only to

God, and releases you from hooks to the past. You see, Satan is a clever fisherman. He knows how to reel you back. Just as he tempted Jesus on the mountaintop with entitlements he knew Jesus deserved, he tempts you to bitterness through the empowering feelings of rage. Satan knows that if you let go, God will heal you and lead you closer to Himself.

Letting go releases your expectations so you go even further. The failure of your marriage wasn't about you being unlovable or unloving. Maybe your ex justified his behavior by accusing you of not meeting his needs or of being lousy in bed. Maybe he loved you as much as he was capable. Letting go of your expectations for him to be courteous, generous, or affectionate allows love and him to be imperfect. You give up faulty beliefs. Your former spouse has no right to define who you are. You no longer need his approval to know what God declares: you are worthy and wonderful.

The fear of the Lord is the only true measure of a woman's worth (Prov. 31:30). You are responsible for simply being faithful—whatever happens. Applaud your friends celebrating anniversaries, but know that neither praying together, worshiping together, or reading Dr. Dobson guarantees love for a lifetime. Though it takes two to keep a covenant, each one of us will stand alone at the Judgment.

Letting go brings you full circle: "You have hedged me behind and before, And laid Your hand upon me . . . . If I ascend into heaven, You are there; if I make my bed in hell, behold, You are there. If I take the wings of the morning, and dwell in the uttermost parts of the sea, Even there Your hand shall lead me…" (Ps. 139:5, 8-10). God doesn't promise to show you the future; He wants to show you Himself. Are you willing to risk a descent into the deep with Him to emerge a woman who is wiser and more beautiful?

The future is so bright it burns my eyes.

∾ Oprah Winfrey

The How of Letting Go

One of divorce's most crucial decisions is discerning how to let go. There are two ways to do it, both necessary at different times:

(1) Physically letting go, getting rid of, throwing away, or carting off.

(2) Emotionally/mentally disengaging from places, people, and possessions, allowing them a different meaning.

Ron Lee Davis said, "I believe you need to be challenged to take responsibility for your own feelings and to take action to assist God in His effort to make you whole."[2]

Your decision about how to let go will be based upon who you know yourself to be and what is at stake. It depends on your expectations about life, whether you are an optimist or a pessimist, what you fear most and what is most important to you.

You may know gut-wrenching fear as you confront the unknown in everything you do, from paying the electric bill or buying a house to watching your health teeter on the edge. Often things go crash, bang, bam all at once. Sometimes you don't have the luxury of mulling over what to keep, what to let go. You make decisions in a split second. Other times, the future stretches endlessly. You want to get something over with, and it gets delayed.

Letting go is inner resolve and dogged determination under stress. You want to do more than cope. Here's help:

• Put into words the choices before you. Write down pros and cons. Be specific. Keep the lists in front of you. Pray over them daily.

• Glean wisdom from many counselors. Can you tap into a church staff? a personal counselor, lawyer, or accountant who charges on a sliding scale? a friend of a friend who has gone through a similar experience?

- Remember there are risks to every choice. No one way is the right way. No one can tell you what is best for you. The responsibility lies on your shoulders. Some people want to stay as safe as possible; others risk more. There are consequences for inaction and a reaction to everything you do. Eventually you must just do it. It's okay, because "underneath are the everlasting arms" (Deut. 33:27).

Relax! You are not responsible
for everything in the universe.
That's still my job. Love, God.

∼ Barbara Johnson

WARNING! FLASHBACKS AHEAD.

It takes courage to go through a divorce. Courage is not putting up a good front, donning a happy face, thinking cheerful thoughts, pretending "all is well." That's just fooling yourself.

When a painful memory bursts upon the scene like a big-mouth eel and bares its razor-sharp teeth, stand your ground. This is a flashback. Shout back at the pain: "Only God has the right to define me. I will not give my ex or my past that power." And pray continually: "Lord, help me hold tightly to your view of me."

When Letting Go Means Keeping It Together

Legacy and family are important to you. How do you relinquish your emotional attachment to things? The day he drove away with half of the furniture, moving it to a place he (and maybe "she") would use, you were devastated. You felt cheated because those things belonged to you. It didn't matter if he had bought them before you married or they had been passed down through his family; they had been incorporated into your family—yours intertwined with his, continuous, extending into the future.

What about the things that remained with you, now tainted with memories? The antiques you purchased on your wedding anniversary? That love seat you saved so long to buy?
You've looked through your wedding album so many times,
cherishing how you met and the funny things that happened
on that day. You'd hoped a daughter would want to wear your
wedding dress, so you'd carefully preserved it.

Through the years, you documented family life in photo
albums and scrapbooks, safekeeping memories of vacations, cele-
brations, and holidays. When he left, not only did he remove
himself, but he obliterated the continuity you took pleasure in
preserving. What you held precious was devalued; you can never
replace it.

C.S. Lewis said, "Relying on God has to begin all over again
every day as if nothing yet had been done."[3] So it is with legacy.
You are what you have experienced and that is what you pass on.
Just because he is no longer in the picture doesn't mean there is
no picture. You are still guardian of family history, keeper of continuity. You have another kind of legacy to give: faithfulness in
adversity, grace under pressure, the comfort of your presence.

"Families come in all shapes," writes Ingrid Trobisch.
"Regardless of configuration, there will always be those individuals who are the home keepers. . . . Each of us shelter springs of
our ancestral legacy, spiritual heritage and personal value which
eventually flow on to those who come after."[4]

Treasure every moment. Document it. Your future comes with
the fortitude to walk into it. Don't let the term "broken family"
cause you to sink into despair. Sometimes letting go means holding on. As you touch the past, you come to terms with it. You
assess its meaning, deciding what to keep and what to let go. You
say, "These pictures are who I was and part of why I am becoming who I am now," and resist tearing them from the pages of the
scrapbook. You may choose to remove photos of him, but keep
his parents' wedding photo there for your children.

Copy this poem and place it on your refrigerator.

EMPTY HANDS

One by one
God took them from me,
All the things
I treasured most,
Until I was empty-handed,
Every glittering toy
was lost.
And I walked
earth's highway grieving
In my rags and poverty
Till I heard
His voice inviting,
"Lift your empty hands
to Me."
So I turned my hands
toward heaven,
And He filled them
with a store
Of His own
transcendent riches
Till they could contain
no more.
And at last
I comprehended,
With my stupid mind
and dull
That God could not pour
His riches
Into hands already full.

Anonymous

Real courage is owning up
to the fact that we face
a terrifying task,
admitting that we are
appropriately frightened,
identifying sources of help
and strength outside
and within ourselves,
and then going ahead
and doing what needs
to be done.

∼ Dr. Alla Renee Bozarth

N: When Dan moved out, I was still reeling with disbelief while he had prepared himself for the ramifications of divorce. He warned me, "We'll have to sell the house."

"How dare you say that!" I responded. "This is my home, and the home of our children!"

Friends wondered why I would want to stay there. "Surely, it must hold painful memories," they said. I saw things differently. Driven by a protective instinct like a mother bear, I determined not to lose our mountain cottage, low-rate mortgage, or the peace I felt on our half acre of ponderosa pines.

I went to a lawyer, and then armed with legal counsel, stood fast on my decision to stay put until our youngest graduated from high school. I brought to Dan's attention that the children deserved stability through their trauma and that selling the house would force us into a cramped place where none of us would feel safe.

Dan agreed. A year later, he said he'd done so out of guilt and again insisted on selling. I stood my ground; the property settlement agreement was final.

But "holding on" to the house has meant "letting go" of emotional associations with Dan. There are reminders of his presence. Each time I rev up the lawn mower, I think of the pride he took maintaining the yard. And when I repair the pickets on the little white fence out front, I can't help remembering the summer he built it and the all-American dream it represented.

In order to move on psychologically in the place I live, I let go—not of the memories themselves—but of the pain associated with them.

I never hated a man enough to give him back his diamonds.

~ Zsa Zsa Gabor

Less Luggage Means a Lighter and Larger Heart

The 1996 movie *The First Wives Club* was labeled by the media as a movie about revenge. But it wasn't. Although the theme involved real emotions of women dumped after long-term marriages, the movie is about what happens beyond betrayal— becoming empowered for ministry. A beau-

LIKE THESE LADIES

You are repositioning yourself for living well, loving much, and laughing more often. You are emptying your hands to hold something new.

Princess Salimah lightened up. The former wife of the richest man in the world, Aga Khan, recently sold $15 million worth of her jewels, including a deep blue, 13.78-carat heart-shaped diamond. Once a top fashion model, the former Sarah Crocker-Poole told Christie's that the jewels no longer go with her new lifestyle.[5]

From the time of her divorce until her death, Princess Diana was in the mode of lightening up. She dug deep into her closet and dumped her dresses. She placed her "working wardrobe" of fabulous gowns worn at official engagements on the auction block at Christie's in New York. The money went to charity. Before the auction, journalist Cathy Horyn commented that Princess Diana's new look, with its "conspicuous absence of geriatric jewels and dowdy royal drapery…gives the impression that the sale of her fabled raiments represents more than closet cleaning. She is jettisoning a life that never was."[6]

PRACTICAL WAYS TO LIGHTEN UP

Shedding is a process. Over the coming months, you'll make decisions about what you are better off without. Cart it off, have a garage sale, or ask a friend to dump it for you. Have a party, and turn letting go into a celebration.

- *Get rid of the clothes you wore with him. Take a couple outfits at a time to a consignment shop and earn enough for something new.*

- *Sell your heavy furniture at a garage sale. Replace it with light pieces you can move easily. (Our editor, Lorraine Davis, says, "This one seems impractical. Can't we just buy those five-dollar furniture-moving casters and spare Grandma's prize credenza?")*

- *Wrap in paper your wedding album and love letters, and any other photographs you no longer want. Shelve them upright, labeled for your children. Schedule an evening to work on new albums with other divorced friends.*

tiful crisis center for women evolved out of heartbreak.

"Don't get mad. Get everything," said Ivana Trump, who played herself in the movie. For the heroines, that meant using everything they learned and received from this disastrous experience to move on and help others do the same. The first wives found a way to laugh while making their experience redemptive.

You, too, can see your heavy experience is waiting to be played with, repositioned, and reorganized. Letting go moves you into healing waters that take you beyond justice to mercy, beyond complacency to compassion, beyond what you thought would destroy you to lightheartedness.

Some days you even chuckle. He is no longer the man who has everything. Why? Because he no longer has you!

Do you see yourself as one who is in some kind of a trial under God's training and for His timing?" asks Joni Eareckson Tada. "Let it be, let it go on, until the Lord deeply imparts in your life a rich and unique message. And then He will open doors and push you through them and let you share what you have learned for others' encouragement and His glory. You just take care to deepen your message. Leave it up to God to broaden it."[7]

Heart Work:

Purchase a helium balloon. Write a brief note about the bitterness you feel, the betrayal you didn't deserve, the truth that can't be vindicated. Tie this to its tail. Instead of stomping on the balloon, take it outside and release it. Watch it float away. It's light and buoyant. You're letting go.

- *Sell the jewelry he bought you if it bothers you. Exchange it at the jewelers, or offer it to your daughters.*

- *Go through books, and give away what reminds you of him. If his handwriting is in a book, but you loved it, buy a new copy.*

- *Get out your camera and shoot photos of your new life. Dress up for photo-ops. Start another album.*

- *Take down everything hanging on the walls, freshen the paint and rehang pictures differently. Create a new look.*

- *Window-shop in catalogs for new dishes or flatware. Clip pictures and glue them into a notebook. Buy one piece occasionally.*

10

My Ticket
Outta Here

Do not say,
"I'll do to him as he has done to me;
I'll pay that man back for what he did."

∼ Proverbs 24:29, NIV

*O*f the many lakes nestled between the shoulders of Oregon's Cascade mountain range, one is particularly serene. At 1,932 feet, Crater Lake is the deepest in the United States. This crystal-blue body of water reflects images like a mirror. You can almost see its bottom. But it wasn't always that way. This peaceful setting is evidence that a fiery eruption, forty-two times greater than Mt. St. Helen's, forever changed the landscape.

Mt. Mazama was once a 12,000-foot-high volcano. Pressure released within the earth fueled a momentous eruption. About 7,700 years ago the cone collapsed in on itself. Volcanic ash covered 5,000 square miles, scattering over an area that would have covered eight states and three Canadian provinces. Smoldering remains molded a caldera, at first too hot to hold water. No stream runs in or out of the basin; the water is replenished with yearly snow melt. Today tourists stand in awe of the beauty of Crater Lake from Rim Village 1,000 feet above, looking down at eagles in flight over its surface.[1]

Divorce is also a reminder of lives changed forever. Internal pressure in the human landscape forces an eruption. Violent energy is released as anger, rage, and thoughts of revenge. Hopes and dreams fail, collapsing in on each other. In the heat of it all, you can't imagine anything positive filling the gaping hole that is left.

Time passes, and inherent in it is the opportunity to convert negative energy into positive, replenishing what once was with something new. Changes in your life create a hollow, waiting to be filled by God, like empty hands. Now there is a way to redeem the losses. That way is forgiveness. It can transform the vacant crater into a calm setting. You clearly mirror forgiveness in a serene and transparent life.

> *From the hollow eyes of death, I spy life peering.*
>
> ~ Shakespeare

What Forgiveness Is

"We can't control others, and we certainly can't force them to be good to us on our terms," says Archibald Hart in *Growing Up Divorced.* "If you have tried your best to effect healing in a relationship…but are unable to make any progress, pack your emotional bags and move on. You cannot limit your recovery because someone else refuses to go along with it….There must come a time, after we have tried everything reasonable to confront our hurt feelings, when we must claim our freedom. It is our God-given right, and our healing depends on it."[2]

But rage and hostility are automatic responses. Malcolm Boyd, an Episcopal minister and author, says the victim is ourselves when we deny our own peace, permitting anger "to burst into a hot flame inside us….Yet we are no more perfect than that hapless person locked in our past."[3] Boyd says that when we are able to forgive, our healing begins.

> *I will not permit any man to narrow and degrade*
> *my soul by making me hate him.*
>
> ~ Booker T. Washington

Forgiveness is a positive response to someone else's problem.

To forgive, you do not need the cooperation of the person who wronged you, because you are saying to him, "I will not own your problem." You see your ex-spouse as human with his own set of hurts. You realize you are no longer responsible for his well-being or the resolution of his issues. You refuse to be hooked and reeled back to the relationship with its tumult of emotions.

> *Always do right—*
> *this will gratify some and astonish the rest.*
>
> ∽ Mark Twain

Forgiveness is reconciliation with the past.

You can never make sense of the past, but you can make peace with it and put it behind you, where it belongs. You can say, "I forgive you, but I don't have to come under your influence. I set you free from the emotional debt. You don't owe me anything. I surrender my right to take revenge." Job said, "I have not allowed my mouth to sin by asking for his life in a curse" (Job 31:30, NASB). Look at it this way: Forgiveness is the sweetest revenge of all.

> *Real forgiveness means looking steadily at the sin,*
> *the sin that is left over without any excuse,*
> *after all allowances have been made,*
> *and seeing it in all its horror,*
> *dirt, meanness and malice,*
> *and nevertheless being wholly reconciled*
> *to the man who has done it.*
>
> ∽ C.S. Lewis

Forgiveness is celebration of your new life.

Forgiveness "frees up the energy you've been devoting to anger," says Dr. Scott Stanley, adjunct associate professor at Fuller Theological Seminary.[4] When feelings become neutralized, bitterness can't harden your spirit and form a crust on your personality. Mental determination coupled with spiritual insight bring you to a place where you no longer react but choose your response.

Old pain may erupt from time to time. Expect it. Remain receptive to God to replenish your spirit. With time, the smoldering embers die out. Long-hidden talents become visible. Dormant dreams start to grow again.

> *Many people lose their tempers*
> *merely from seeing you keep yours.*
>
> ◦ Frank Moore Colby

What Forgiveness Is Not

Forgiveness is not forgetting.
To forgive does not mean you pretend the inappropriate behavior of another person never happened. It is not feigning amnesia about the hurt and saying, "Perhaps it wasn't as bad as I remember." That is rationalization or denial. Forgiveness makes conscious moral discernments in full sight of the truth. You remember the injury but no longer react to the pain. It does not mean you become Milquetoast.

> *Hating people is like burning down*
> *your own house to get rid of a rat.*
>
> ◦ Harry Emerson Fosdick

Forgiveness is not giving the other person power to hurt you again.
A woman who has experienced physical, emotional, or verbal abuse from her former spouse may feel more in control if she does not forgive him. But unforgiveness offers false protection by setting up a boundary of resentment that is unhealthy.

"For a long time, I thought my lack of forgiveness of my ex-husband was my strength," says Ginger. After a car accident placed him in a coma and led to his death, Ginger realized his humanity. "I felt safe after he died because he was no longer in a position to hurt me," she admits. "Before that I was afraid forgiving meant I would be expected to go back to him."

> *A woman who can't forgive*
> *should never have more than a nodding acquaintance*
> *with a man.*

~ Ed Howe

Forgiveness is not a feeling.

"The one thing I haven't done is forgive Ted," says Meg, nine years divorced. "And I know I can't move on with my life until I do." Right now Meg does not feel forgiving toward the man who physically beat her, but she's determined to become willing to forgive, not for his well-being but for hers. Her willingness is the first and most important step. Like love and commitment, forgiveness is an acting out of what you believe is right in spite of how you feel.

> *Our true safety lies in learning to forgive one another.*
> *Forgiveness is the most radical way*
> *of moving beyond the law of history....*
> *We can never begin anything new without forgiveness.*

~ Sam Keen

Forgiveness is not about him but about you.

A forgiving spirit leaves you with a clean heart and open hands. Unforgiveness snuffs out the spiritual fuel that propels you forward. Psalm 66:18 says the Lord doesn't listen if you "cherish" sin in your heart (NIV). To forgive is to obey God by giving Him first priority in your life. Forgiveness says: *Lord God, You are more important than anything my ex-husband has done to me. I'm willing to no longer keep score of wrongs. I need healing more than I want revenge for the hurt.*

MY PRAYER OF
FORGIVENESS
            by Kari West

When you're ready, pray this prayer when you need to, inserting into the blanks the name of the one who hurt you. Little by little, with willingness, this prayer will move from your head into your heart. Eventually you'll feel it and mean it. Forgiveness is your ticket out of here.

_____'s Father, Who art in heaven, hallowed be Thy name. Thy kingdom come and Thy will be done in ___'s life here on earth as if ____ were sitting beside You in heaven. Give _____ what he needs today to sustain his life. Forgive the sins ____ has committed and help ____ to forgive others. Don't test ____ beyond what he can bear. Like me, ____ is weak. And please keep _____ safe from the Evil One. May ____ find peace and joy in Your kingdom.

It is easier to forgive an enemy than to forgive a friend.

∼ William Blake

Forgiveness is never easy.

Unforgiveness feeds on your fear of admitting and addressing your own bitter, critical spirit. Forgiveness is an act of the will, a declaration you won't take revenge anymore. That doesn't mean the pain goes away. It is tough before it is tender. If this is your first attempt at forgiving, expect resistance. You are going against the grain when you decide to quit blaming another person who harmed you and when you stop wanting him to make it up to you.

People don't trip over mountains, they stumble on stones.

∼ Old Saying

K: After I'd settled into my house, I figured the next step was simple: Just forgive Ed—until The Neighbor shared what Ed had told her that prior Christmas: That he served me with papers and sold the house out from under me; they needed to lie low because he had me just where he wanted me; I was ready to sign away everything.

Did I want to forgive Ed? No. Did I feel forgiving? Of course not. Instead, I determined to step beyond my feelings with an act of my will and allow the Lord to teach me forgiveness. At first, I couldn't pray for Ed. Then I started reading aloud a paraphrase of the Lord's Prayer (see sidebar this page), accomplishing what I could not do myself—surrendering my will.

Today I no longer read aloud that prayer, but I still do the hard work of cleaning up my feelings when I'm attacked by Ed. I still struggle against defending myself. I battle wanting "to be right" with needing "to be whole." Control feels more about righting wrongs than turning the other cheek. It's difficult to achieve the standard Jesus set. He didn't justify himself. He didn't take revenge. He didn't accept or excuse sin. He forgave.

The process of forgiveness never ends. Each year brings other insults and assaults—real or imagined—that force me to face personal obstacles within and without: irrational guilt over my inability to keep family together; justifiable anger over a loss of justice; a volatile mix of past hurt, present harassment, and the possibility of future hostility.

For me, forgiveness is not forgetting what happened. The photo albums from the years of our marriage are still intact. Forgiveness is not accepting or tolerating Ed's behavior; it's not changing it either. I can't. Forgiveness is what God does in me after I relinquish my right to pay Ed back with what I think he deserves.

Help me forgive _____'s deception and betrayal, and the pain, frustration, and disappointment he brought to me. Help me forgive him for the financial concerns, anxiety, sleepless nights, loneliness, confusion, humiliation, and other problems _____ caused in my life because of his breaking covenant with You long before his infidelity to me.

Forgive me for my anger, rage, and hateful thoughts, and my part in causing our marriage to fail. Thy will be done in my life. Thy will be done in _____'s life. Amen.

Adapted from the Lord's Prayer (Matt. 6)

No revenge is more honorable than the one not taken.

∽ Spanish Proverb

N: "You need to forgive me," Dan said. "If you stay bitter, you'll only end up hurting yourself." That kind of patronization made the forgiveness process more complicated for me. *Did Dan think I trusted him and would accept his advice? Was he saying this just to humiliate me further? Should I forgive because it was the spiritually correct thing to do? What is real here?* I wondered.

Chris Darden, O.J. Simpson's prosecutor, was seen on TV standing in front of the microphones at a press conference after the trial. He said, "I'm not angry. I'm not bitter..." Then, starting another sentence he stopped, looked down, and walked away. Later, he admitted, "I walked away from the mike rather than lie." Like Darden, I knew, above everything, I had to be true.

There was a time when anger was the only justifiable response to what happened. I even ripped pictures of Dan out of the scrapbooks. The time came to move beyond, not because of what Dan said, but in spite of it. Forgiveness became a journey that is unhurried. At first I could only pray, "Lord, Dan doesn't deserve it and I don't feel like it, but I forgive him." Each day I pray to forgive at least 1 percent more, but I don't have to keep worrying about whether I've forgiven or not.

I told Dan, "I am forgiving by degrees. I'm not there 100 percent, but I'm on my way." I am not giving up my moral discernment, but I am giving up my coldness toward him. With time, I'll be able to give up the stiff-arming I use to keep him at an emotional distance.

I keep offering God my spirit and asking Him to keep the channel between Him and me pure. Forgiveness is helping me complete the work of separation; to honor the place where my marriage hit a wall, like placing a cross at a roadside spot where someone died in an accident. Just as I continually recommitted to love in my marriage, I am continually recommitting to forgive in my divorce.

> *Always forgive your enemies—*
> *nothing annoys them so much.*
>
> ∼ Oscar Wilde

How to Forgive

You are standing on the ridge between Bitter and Better. This rugged crossing will appear again. Forgiveness is not a one-time option. It's an ongoing choice. When a letter from your former spouse stirs up the ashes or a phone call pummels your peace of mind, it may feel like the past has a stranglehold on you. Forgiveness negates its power. It is never too late to change course and get back on track. Here's how:

Adopt an attitude to forgive.

At first, forgiveness requires that you discipline your mind and spirit. This decision is one of the most courageous you will ever make. Project yourself into the future. Decide what would make you feel as if you had dealt honorably with him. Then do that.

Resolve not to retaliate, but speak with grace about your mate wherever possible. Take a mental break from anger. A vacation from hostility. A recess from rage. Gradually, you'll release the poison. With practice, you'll experience entire days or weeks of serenity. Relish them. But don't beat yourself up when anger reignites.

Forgive us our debts, as we forgive our debtors.

⌒ Matthew 6:12

Be motivated by the eternal.

Dare to pray for the one who hurt you. Release him to God's mercy and judgment. If you need to, use the Lord's Prayer as a pattern (or a paraphrase, like the one on page 150) and read it over and over. You may have to do it mechanically at first.

Accept the empowering of the Holy Spirit. "He is our engagement ring for the wedding feast of the Lamb," says Dr. Larry Vold, pastor of The Neighborhood Church, Castro Valley, California. We're promised that the Bridegroom will return. In the meantime, the Holy Spirit acts as our guarantee and stirs our hope. Open yourself to His comfort in His love.

Resist temptation as Jesus did on the desert mountain. Fling Satan's torments back. Put on the whole armor of God (Eph. 6:10-18). Pray Jesus' blood over the doorposts of your mind, as the Israelites did in Egypt during the plague (Ex. 12:23).

> *Lord, if you keep in mind our sins*
> *then who can ever get an answer to his prayers?*
> *But you forgive! What an awesome thing this is!*
>
> ～ Psalm 130:3, 4, TLB

Be patient with yourself.

No one says you have to accomplish forgiveness all at one time. Allow yourself to get over it by increments. Just be willing to be willing; let God keep track of the progress. Keep at the hard work of letting go and moving on, even when the fire of anger re-ignites.

Just as it is easier to turn on a light than it is to drive out the darkness, give joy a chance. Let new experiences happen. Make appreciation and thanksgiving a vital part of every day. Keep wondering, *What is around the corner?*

> *The weak can never forgive.*
> *Forgiveness is the attribute of the strong.*
>
> ～ Mahatma Gandhi

Homegrown Rituals

Divorce doesn't allow for burying of the dead because both parties go on living. There is no ritual to honor your sacred pain. Ghosts haunt those left behind and hover over future decisions: at graduations, weddings, the birth of grandchildren. Personal rituals of forgiveness settle these emotional issues. They take skeletons from closets, put them in the ground where they belong, and bring closure.

There is no public or private ceremony to mourn the passing of a marriage. A death certificate, entitled "The Final Decree," is filed at the county courthouse, but no memorial service is held when your dearly departed exits your life. Nobody brings over casseroles or stays to cry with you. The pastor gives no eulogy or assurance of life after death. There is no ceremony, no headstone, and no beautifully ribboned bouquets.

There is life after the death of a love.

∾ Kari

K ∘ Since I did not contest my divorce, my appearance was not required in the courtroom. On legal documents, my signature, that of my ex, and the judge's verified the end of the marriage. I marked the passage alone. No one at work knew the significance of that sunny summer day; it was business as usual.

But my divorce was a death. I needed to erect a tombstone on the grave of my marriage—a memorial to acknowledge that I had belonged to somebody for twenty-two years. Ed received this note, prepared in advance and timed to arrive that day:

> *To the memory of a love that began one snowy Christmas;*
> *To a marriage that saw a young man's dreams of family and college degrees come true.*
> *To a marriage that saw a beautiful baby daughter born to a young woman who wanted nothing more than to be a loving wife and mother.*
> *To the memory of what could have been, in sickness and in health, for richer or poorer, "forsaking all others, until death we do part."*
> *May you now find whatever it is (or whoever) really makes you happy. I do wish you well!*

Each word was carefully chosen. It was a love note to my suffering and a thank-you for what was good. It was a way to say good-
bye to the me who was Ed's wife, the me who trusted him once
upon a time. It was good-bye to the physical, emotional, and spiritual intimacy I thought we once shared, to our joint history, the
common ground, traditions, and goals—fulfilled and unful-
filled—we had shared. I was closing the back cover of the volume
on my marriage. My feelings were an odd mix. I wanted to
remember what was good. That's what forgiveness is all about.

Visit the Cemetery

If you haven't scheduled the funeral, what are you waiting for?
Finish the chapter. Bury the dead. Reclaim the good, and redeem
the bad. Memorialize your loss. Toss out the roses and trinkets.
Kick at the dirt, if you feel like it. Wish your former spouse well.
Then walk on.

And in quiet moments, when you are alone, thinking no one
cares, remember that the most important guest at any funeral
stands beside you each time you weep.

> *But Mary was standing outside the tomb*
> *weeping....She turned around, and beheld Jesus*
> *standing there, and did not know that it was Jesus.*
> *Jesus said to her, "Woman, why are you weeping?*
> *Whom are you seeking?"*

~ John 20:11, 15, NASB

N: I spent this Easter in Jerusalem on assignment. I'd been
asked to write about the resurrection, how walking in
Jesus' footsteps is a new beginning every day. *Yeah, right!* I thought,
remembering previous trips to Israel: The first, two years before I
married, when I started praying for a man after God's heart instead
of the man of my dreams. The second trip, two years before my
divorce, I awoke troubled one night. I prayed for several hours for
our marriage, believing God was restoring our love.

"She was weeping." The speaker's words at the Garden Tomb Easter sunrise service pulled me back to the present. "Mary was brokenhearted," he said. *This trip I want to bury the last vestiges of bitterness toward Dan,* I thought, *but how? I want God to prepare me to love again, but can I trust Him?*

Then I realized Mary must have felt let down, too. Her friend, the man she'd believed to be the Son of God, the Messiah, was dead. In His darkest hour, tortured beyond recognition, He'd proclaimed words of forgiveness—despite the pain, abandonment, and rejection. Was that divinity? Or stupidity? Was it love or spiritual impotence?

"Mary knew a mixture of hopeless longing and sorrow," the speaker continued. "She'd brought spices to lay around His body, now decaying, or so she thought. She wanted only to be with the one she loved."

Sitting in the garden that day, in the emptiness of divorce, I felt disappointed, the way Mary did finding the tomb vacant. She'd turned and looked around in the hazy dawn. "Whom are you seeking?" someone asked, but she didn't recognize the man.

Just feet from where they may have stood, I heard twittering in a fig tree. Two small finches swooped down and flitted playfully. Beyond them, a white half-moon faded into the pale sky. Bells from the Church of the Holy Sepulcher clanged. The finches disappeared. Above my head, a blackbird took their place. It warbled a most amazing song.

"Jesus said one word: 'Mary!'"

This Easter at sunrise, it was as if He said my name, too. I was merely bringing spices to a marriage already dead. He had an encounter with resurrection in mind.

"The one who loves will always find what she is looking for," the speaker concluded. As light fell over a garden in Jerusalem, the seeds of forgiveness I'd sown led beyond healing.

> **If I keep a green bough in my heart,**
> **the singing bird will come.**
>
> ∼ Chinese Proverb

Forever Changed

In the landscape of your life, God is creating transparent lakes out of the violent, explosive experience of loss. It appears to be the opposite of what you've hoped and prayed for. Can anything beautiful come out of so much disgrace? You doubt it. Yet under the simmering cinders, grace is His intent. You will never look at anything quite the same. With hindsight, someday you'll see His mercy in the madness, His peace in the process. For now, forgiveness is what takes you there.

11

I Am Going To Make It

For I called him alone,
And blessed him and increased him.

∼ Isaiah 51:2

*I*n solitude, on the Eastern side of the Sierras, stands the oldest living tree on earth: the 4,600-year-old bristlecone pine, Methuselah. As enduring as the Egyptian pyramids, it is testimony to toughness and resilience. Flourishing with a minimum of moisture, its roots sink into solid dolomite rock. What makes this tree survive also makes it beautiful. Gnarled and wind-twisted, its trunk grows into curved and irregular patterns, flexing with weather that includes a history of glacial ice flows. Resistant to disease, the bristlecone produces heavy amounts of pitch that ward off insects and decay.

Bristlecone pines are not sheltered in groves or forests. They grow in desolate locations at an elevation of 10,000 feet, near the timberline, where nothing else can. Stark and alone, they stand against the open sky.

What lies behind us and what lies before us
are tiny matters compared to what lies within us.

∽ Ralph Waldo Emerson

Rooted in Ancient Rock

Too often divorce thrusts women into what feels like exile in life's remote, rugged timberline. Isolated. Cut off from the refreshment of relationships. Too much solitude. Too much history—and aging by the minute! But your roots, like the pitons of a mountain climber or the roots of the bristlecone are sinking tenaciously into ancient rock.

Pat answers and clichés don't work after divorce. You must think beyond the paradigms in a way people who have not gone through it would never dare. "Americans are brought up on the fiction that there is always a happy ending—or at least, there ought to be," says psychologist Sonya Friedman. "Sitcoms, in which problems are presented and neatly solved within half an hour, hammer this message home every night. Real life, however, doesn't work that way."[1]

It's not just television and movies. There are times you would rather not go to church. It makes you feel the same way, as if all things are supposed to work out just fine if you love God. And what if they don't work out just fine? You're left alone in the church pew, wondering: *Didn't I pray enough? have enough faith? read enough Scripture?*

In formerly familiar social and spiritual settings, you now feel like a round peg in a square hole. The world says, "Bloom where you're planted" or "Get a life!" The church says, "Wait on God" and "Keep your hope." But how do you handle the disorientation and isolation? You feel there's got to be more to life after divorce than continuing with the same ol' same ol', heeding advice of family and friends who have never stood exposed and naked as you. You sense they don't want to hear about it.

You're ready for a new level of faith. You know the only way is up and out in the open.

> ***Stand firm in all the will of God,***
> ***mature and fully assured.***
>
> ～ Colossians 4:12, NIV

Seeking a State of Grace

"People who don't climb mountains tend to assume the sport is a reckless, Dionysian pursuit," says Jon Krakauer, who witnessed the deaths of three people on Mt. Everest, the highest spot on earth. "I quickly came to understand that climbing was primarily about enduring pain....It struck me that most of us were probably seeking, above all else, something like a state of grace."[2]

Krakauer's insights into this state of grace for mountain climbers are enlightening as a metaphor for divorce. Above 18,000 feet, the simple act of survival is difficult. The air is thin, brain cells die, thinking becomes confused, circulation slows, and movements become sluggish. Sleeping and eating are almost impossible. In the extreme cold, frostbite always threatens. Krakauer is critical of guided expeditions because they lead to a lack of personal responsibility, with the leader making all the decisions. Dependence on one person, he says, leads to lapses in judgment.

Climbing in a group does give a sense of camaraderie and support, especially in the beginning; but when push comes to shove, it is a solitary climb. Some turn back, some pass ahead of you, but whether or not you make it is solely up to your wits and stamina, and God's grace.

Beck Weathers' name was nearly added to the list of eight climbers who lost their lives on May 10, 1996—the most fatalities recorded in one day on Mt. Everest. Fifteen hundred feet below the summit, when Beck's vision blurred, his guide insisted he wait to be picked up on the way back. However, the guide died further on. Eventually, Beck joined a small group on the descent in plunging temperatures. But for Beck, "the lights went out."[3] Unconscious, he was left on the mountainside, because, Beck explains, "I was in a hypothermic coma. Nobody comes back from that."

After Beck was lying fifteen hours on the ice, his brain began to stir. He struggled up and shuffled blindly into the wind. "I was absolutely certain I was dead," he says. Miraculously, Beck stumbled into camp. Astonished climbers tucked him into a shelter with a hot water bottle. He heard them radioing base camp, referring to him as "dead guy in the tent." But early the next morning,

Beck emerged, somehow finding that state of grace that had eluded eight others.

Where do you find the fortitude and resolve to get up one more time the way Beck Weathers did? How do you weather the worst to keep going?

"Everything in life offers opportunity," says Sonya Friedman, "if not always for hope, then for knowledge. Learning to accept that suffering hardship is part of life is perhaps the keystone of maturity. Coming to terms with this fact ultimately makes it possible for us to become women of substance." She continues, "It allows us to tolerate the vicissitudes of life with more resilience and understanding than we ever thought possible. It means accepting pain in our lives without inflicting it on ourselves or others."[4]

But not everyone finds this place so easily. There are casualties. One Christian woman said, "I'm still praying for a healing so I can trust again. It's been over six years, and I'm as afraid of intimacy now as the day we separated. Kind of frightening how protective I've become of my fragile little heart. I've been told the fortress I've built around me is so tight and strong, even the kindest, most gentle and honest gentleman couldn't begin to break through."

Like the professional guided expeditions on Mt. Everest, the unaware church often leaves its own wounded to die slow, icy deaths. Bible studies on marriage are usually taught from an idealistic singular viewpoint, assuming both parties are committed to lifelong marriage.

There is no preparation for the possibility that one partner—even a Christian, even the one you believed God led you to—may have a hidden agenda or character defect. God does not always keep us safe. Praying together does not guarantee staying together. Too often a divorced Christian is invisible in the church, misplaced and without identity.

"Human failing is a reality of Christian experience, even among God's choicest men and women," says Dwight Small, professor emeritus of Westmont College. "But God's grace is redemptive and restorative. So we adhere to the divinely ordained norm for marriage with full commitment, and we hold high the ideal. But if the ideal is missed and a failed marriage results, then we, as responsible ministers of God, must help broken and hurting individuals find the best possibilities in God's abundant provision."[5]

K: "You are born alone, you live alone, and you die alone," my mother always said. I never understood her words until Ed left. I had deluded myself that "being" the right person, as my childhood Sunday School teacher had said, was more important than finding the right person. Trying to be a Proverbs 31 woman, I'd looked after my household, earned a living, and even worked with my hands—sewing drapes, making my clothes and Melanie's, raising vegetables, making jam, winning blue ribbons at the county fair for my knitting and crochet work.

But my love, integrity, effort, and faith could not keep my marriage together. I had depended upon another human being to always be there, when he may not have been capable of lifelong commitment. Nothing had prepared me for that possibility.

More recently, I discovered how repulsive that seven-letter D-word is in the Christian community.

When Noelle and I appeared on a Christian radio broadcast, there was negative response from several listeners decrying the fact that the program hosted two divorced women.[6] "That's just the point," we said. "We are evidence divorce cannot be avoided sometimes, regardless of how much we wish it could."

Don't people get it? we wondered.

The Divorce Dilemma

After interviewing a random selection of adults nationwide, half of whom were born-again Christians, the Barna Research Group found that born-again Christians are slightly more likely to go through a divorce (27% vs. 23% of non-Christians).

Those who describe themselves as Christian fundamentalists are even more likely to get divorced (30%). With data that shows accepting Christ does not reduce the incidence of divorce, Barna concludes that the Christian community must re-examine the ways in which family matters are addressed within church ministries.

Solving the divorce dilemma is one of the urgent, critical issues facing today's church. Not only how to prevent it, but what to do with adults devastated by it and children growing up in divorced families.[7]

Divorce takes its toll; please have exact change.

∼ Noelle

N: One evening in church, the pastor asked the congregation to pray for people sitting at home who may be considering suicide. I thought, *Why not admit there is pain within the church, not just outside it? There are people sitting in this very congregation right now in so much pain they have thought of suicide.* I was one of them, but I didn't say a word because everybody still had their Sunday masks on, including me.

Months later, the pastor asked the congregation to name what they were grateful for. The first woman to speak said, "God healed my marriage." Everyone cheered, "Hallelujah! Praise God!" Since by that time I'd accepted the truth about my former spouse, I felt like raising my hand. I wanted to say, "He delivered me from my marriage." I wonder: *Would the congregation have cheered? Would the pastor have kept his smile?*

A fool sees not the same tree that a wise man sees.

∼ William Blake

Life in Exile: Still Seeking Grace in the Church

Sociologists have studied the reaction of the church to divorce. Dr. Ray DeVries, associate professor of sociology at Westmont

College, in Santa Barbara, California, says, "The church simply does not know what to do with you [divorced people]. You are walking manifestations of our uncertainty." DeVries explains that traditional religions have difficulty facing the modern world because modernity changes religion, even the safe world of evangelicalism. "We are becoming more secular in that we are increasingly rational, private and civil, leaving us confused about our identity."[8]

DeVries says the church is asking, "We are called apart from the world, so how can we accept you? If we accept you, won't others be encouraged to get divorced?" He claims people who are divorced bear the brunt of evangelicals' ambivalence about accommodating the modern world. "We're not sure how much accommodation is too much. We constantly juggle the doctrines of creation, the fall and redemption. But we have a tendency to focus on the fall. We become legalistic because the human response to the fall is to construct careful codes to live by."[9]

"The doctrine of redemption offers a different message," DeVries claims. "If we focus on redemption, we emphasize grace. Perhaps divorce needs to be seen as a manifestation of God's grace rather than as a violation of our legalism."[10]

> If you would like to learn more about the theological viewpoints on divorce and/or remarriage, read: *Divorce and Remarriage, Four Christian Views,* H. Walter House, editor, (Downers Grove, Ill.: InterVarsity Press, 1990).

If you have children, you know too well that divorce has residual effects the church has yet to address. Statistician George Barna found "that within two years after divorce, most single parents abandon the Christian church because they sense condemnation and rejection." The effect divorce has on the generation that is paying for the sins of its fathers, Barna says, "is not a pretty picture."[11]

"The effect of the parents' divorce is played and replayed throughout the first three decades of the children's lives," says Judith Wallerstein, who studied 130 children from 60 marriages for 25 years. "We selected well educated, middle-to-upper class parents for the study," she says, "because we wanted to see divorce under the best of circumstances." Wallerstein's findings, presented at the second World Congress on Family Law and the Rights of Children & Youth in San Francisco in 1997, revealed an adult's experience reaches a peak at breakup and levels off, but the effects of divorce on children are cumulative and increase over time.[12]

N: My older daughter displayed great resilience and diplomacy with both her parents as we navigated divorce. She was my strength and, I also think, her father's. I was grateful for the maturity she exemplified to me and in front of her sisters.

Then one night she broke down at my bedside and cried. "Now I'm always going to be afraid Todd [her longterm boyfriend] will leave me," she said. My spirit sank. I knew that, but I had never expected her to articulate what Wallerstein writes about. "Children of divorce feel the lack of a template for a loving, enduring and moral relationship between a man and a woman," Wallerstein says. "As their anxieties peak throughout society, the full legacy of the past twenty years will begin to hit home."[13]

Forgive us for turning our churches into private clubs …
for pasting stained glass on our eyes and ears
to shut out the cry of the hungry
and the hurt of the world.

∼ A 1968 Litany for Holy Communion,
United Presbyterian Church

K: Nobody knew the obstacles I faced getting Melanie to go to church in the first place. I had to overcome her dad's negative innuendos on top of normal teenage resistance. All I had asked was that she show up once a week until she graduated from high school. It was her choice whether she chose church, Sunday School, or Wednesday-night youth group. She went willingly—until a particular Sunday School discussion turned critical of divorce. Embarrassed, Melanie admitted her parents were divorced. "Wasn't twenty-two years enough?" she sobbed.

Later she snarled at me, "See if I ever go back to church again." Today, her attendance is sporadic. I'm both grieved and outraged at the family of God's insensitivity—until I recall my former "I'll never be divorced" attitude.

> **We must not make assumptions about God's love based on the way people love.**
>
> ❧ Dr. Paul Meier

Take It to Heart

Perhaps these letters to a women's magazine may encourage you to grace fellow climbers. "Thank you for reaffirming the truth that there is struggle in the Christian walk. I long to know the One who is 'Not afraid to touch your hurts.' I have so many! I have become numb from hoping someday God will remember me, too. Cynical? A little. Bitter? Somewhat. Real? Absolutely. But this is where I am and if I am ever going to meet my God, it will be right here. Where it hurts."[14]

"When I feel overwhelmed, I read the article [about divorce] again....It gives me comfort and strength. Thank you for printing a wonderfully insightful, brutally honest real-life story."[15]

"[In] the article...you spoke that ugly word—divorce—out into the light and it didn't contaminate, but helped me see that I still can be a woman of virtue."[16]

That is where you are right now—a woman of virtue, human and divine. God calls you to reality living: an out-in-the-open struggler built for the climb. Tap into your resources. Get gritty. Meet life with wind in your hair. Tell the truth. Reality is not about rigidity but about being grounded in your faith, taking life as it comes. You ordered mercy, but God delivered grace. You are not a delicate hothouse plant tucked under a porch. Now you are enduring the cold. You know living fully is not about rescue but resolve. Jesus has overcome death, divorce, and whatever else you face.

> *Empathy is the human reflection of the incarnation....*
> *We possess the ability to enter*
> *the pain and joy of others.*
>
> ∼ Dr. Dan Allender

Gnarls Mark the Storms

Stability is not about where you live, who you're with, or what you own. Stability lies within you—an invisibly rooted mental fortitude and emotional well-being that draws nourishment from the Rock of Ages.

"As we get older...we come to love the gnarls that mark the storms that have been weathered and the scars that give silent testimony to suffering born with dignity," writes Sam Keen. "The presence of evil may break the heart, but it does not prove the cosmos is a loveless place. To the contrary, sacrilege helps us locate the sacred because when confronted by torture or desecration, we know life should not be violated."[17]

The paradox and the power is that endurance and perseverance turn loneliness and fear upside down. Endurance and perseverance are "qualities we would all like to possess," says Jerry Bridges, "but we are loathe to go through the process that produces them." Bridges says *endurance* is the ability to stand up under adversity; *perseverance* is the ability to progress in spite of it.[18] These qualities enable you to become a woman of substance. being alone again carves a unique groove of approachability. You have been there! You know how *alone* feels.

Next time you meet an elegant lady standing alone on the timberline, let your echo carry far. Shout, "Hey, *there's* a great lover if I ever saw one. She stands with grace. She's living fully and loving well. She's making it." Then tell the world, "Guess what, I'm going to make it, too!"

> *. . . They are so weak that*
> *the wind can carry them off!*
> *A breath can puff them away.*
> *But he [she] who trusts in me*
> *shall possess the land*
> *and inherit my holy mountain.*
>
> ∼ Isaiah 57:13, TLB

P. S. *You* are going to make it!

12

It's Time
To Thrive

*Love…bears all things, believes all things,
hopes all things, endures all things.
Love never fails.*

~ 1 Corinthians 13:4,7-8

N: Early one morning on our first summer vacation without Dan, I went beachcombing with one of my daughters. Along the Pacific shore we saw a sign: Life in the Crash Zone: *Wind against sea creates friction, causing waves to crest, then break with fury against the shore. Anything that finds itself in this crash zone has to hide out or hang on for dear life.*

No one could have better described my life. I thought of Cynthia in the movie *The First Wives Club*, who jumped over a penthouse balcony after her husband walked out. If I had not hung on for dear life, might I have crashed the way she did?

I hoped my future would unfold as blossom petals do in those high-speed science films. I'd been through the hibernation and the crazy get-out-and-go-girl stages. I'd prayed my heart out. I'd journaled my brains out. A whole shelf of dog-eared notebooks under my bed is testimony to that.

Encouragement came in smatterings. And like Cynthia, I got over my ex but found loneliness the long-term killer. What was I supposed to do when my teenagers split in all directions? My best friend was dating, my married friends stayed home, the Christian singles group was flakey, and local nightspots were just the places I'd meet people like my ex and The Neighbor. A family member, tired of my whining, communicated, "Move away or shut up about it."

At the beach, I was thinking about the uncertainty that could put me over the edge; then I read the last phrase on the sign: *Yet a multitude of fragile life thrives right here in the crash zone.*

175

Thrive? I'd hoped just to survive. That day I decided to dig my toes deep into the foamy sand of the beach I'd been cast upon: I would refuse to fade away. I vowed not to disappear or crack up. I was determined not only to endure, but to flourish, succeed, shine.

Look at your feet. You are standing in the sky.

~ Diane Ackerman

Surf the Stops, Starts, and Surprises

Thriving after divorce is surging forward, tugging backward. You are alive and breathing in a restless, shifting sea. Like coral reefs enduring a pounding environment, you have to will to thrive.

You will find that nothing on this earth can propel you toward the future and away from a toxic past faster than enthusiasm. It will cause you to stabilize right where you are and then go somewhere different. If you keep doing things the way you've always done them, you'll never have more than you've always had, or be more than you've always been. If you want to change your life, you've got to build on changes within yourself. The pivotal point is the quality and degree of your ardent fervor for life.

"How can I?" you ask. "After what happened to me!"

It's not that hard. You decide when you want to feel enthusiastic. You decide how impassioned you want to feel. You decide and you determine just how dramatically you will let exuberance change your patterns of behavior, your outlook on circumstances, your charge into the future. Will you open your arms and become infatuated with life or keep them clutched over your breast, withdrawn and afraid? Today, you can make one change. You may as well, for the past is no longer an option.

"Let's face it," says Dory Hollander, "when you've traveled a path strewn with evasive deceptions, lies of exclusivity, broken promises, and a deliberate avoidance of straight and honest talk, it really is time for a change.... However, changing partners won't be enough. If you're sick of what you've been putting up with, you have to consider changing the only person you truly can change—yourself."[1]

If you adapted to him for all those years, now do it for you. Adaptation in the name of love is part of a woman's repertoire from the beginning. You are brought up to respond and surrender: time, energy, affection, your body in love-making. You anticipate needs and respond to them, promising you'll be there.

You pay an enormous price for this twenty-four-hour on-call availability. Your boundaries blur by overlapping responsibilities. On the job you wonder about your child at day care and plan dinner in your mind. At home, you iron both your clothes and the family's, catch up on paperwork, make dentist appointments. Your personal fuel tank often runs on empty. When you think back, can you recall your former spouse pressing your blouse or dicing veggies for the Crock Pot before he left for work? (If so, please write us. We want to know your secret.)

You had geared up to continue to adapt for what was supposed to happen at this time of life, but wildly divergent changes were forced upon you. Now is the time to respond to the hunger of your own soul.

A [wo]man is not old until regrets take the place of dreams.

~ John Barrymore

K . My garden thrives not because it's in a tropical zone or on a level piece of ground—it's neither of these. It exists because it tolerates extremes: scorching sunlight, mildew-generating fog, an irrigation well that often runs dry, and hungry gophers chomping at roots.

"I'm amazed how that hill has responded to your touch; your faith was great," my mother said, describing the steep, arid

California hillside I turned into a lush habitat. It shelters not only fruit, flowers, and vegetables, but wildlife. A variety of birds, butterflies, raccoons, skunks, foxes, and reptiles find sanctuary there.

Mother is right. Tackling slopes, stubborn clay, and hilltop winds takes gutsy faith—both in my garden and my life. It is hard to believe that the thriving woman I am today once journaled: "God, there isn't enough strength anymore to hang onto Your promises. I'm on the brink, ready to crack up." Often I thought I had wasted the best years of my life on Ed.

But it isn't true. Thriving isn't about an ideal location, perfect timing, or climate control. It's happening now as I endure opposition and refuse to give up—whatever I face. As much as I want my life to be a tropical vacation, friction is here to stay. When the gopher turns my flower beds into a war zone, either I slam the gate never to return or I figure he was there first. I endure his rototilling because it makes my digging easier, aerates the packed soil, and unearths surprises, like castoff pieces of flagstone fit for a footpath.

Sure, I rail at life's unfairness, such as my daughter's depression as she struggles with the past. What rubs against me creates heat. But more often than not, friction's heat drives my resolve to sling open life's gate and brave the elements one more time. Besides, I don't want to miss a great garden that's on the grow.

Exceeding Abundantly Beyond

Surprise yourself!

Say *Yes!* to opportunities instead of thinking, *Oh, I couldn't do that!* Come up with one or two snappy aspirations, and trust El Shaddai to bring along the means and ways if He wills it. Dare to believe He does. Unless you have evidence to the contrary, believe that your burning desire was placed there by Him. Look as far into the future as you can, for it is all yours. Within the possibilities of faith are all you long to be and all you long to do.

Practice boomerang joy.

Boomerang joy is something author Barbara Johnson loves to talk about. Sharing boomerang joy means you'll be more playful, give more compliments, and conceive at least one idea a day to cheer someone else. You learn to do random acts of kindness with panache.

Maintain a professional distance from the devil.

As you decide to be enthusiastic and go for God's gusto, that's exactly when Satan is going to show up and try every trick in the book to pop your balloon, rain on your parade, and take away your sugar bread. Be like Martin Luther, who woke up one night in fright, opened his eyes, and saw the devil standing at the end of his bed: "Oh, it's only you," he said calmly, as he turned over and went back to sleep. Don't let fear attach you to the devil.

Make the most of the fact that well-being attracts.

When asked to list what attracted or repelled him as a single man meeting women, Kari's husband, Richard, said he wasn't attracted to women who were preoccupied with their own healing, exhibited a "poor me" attitude, or made gender specific comments, like "All men are jerks!" (even in joking). Those he liked and wanted to know better were women who showed a positive attitude and were outgoing, curious, stimulated by new ideas, and able to converse on a variety of topics. Your vitality is a magnet for friends and opportunities.

It's kind of fun to do the impossible.
∼ Walt Disney

N: At an official Pithy Pity Party I attended, one woman who had also been dumped said she'd given up worrying about her body. "Who cares anyway?" she said. I was flabbergasted and thought, *How could she not care?* Being healthy and fit is more important to me than ever. I drink a lot of water to hydrate my skin and exercise aerobically three to four times a week. Feeling good creates momentum to look good, and looking good motivates me to be more outgoing and friendly.

But all the makeup in the world doesn't substitute for lack of twinkle. That's why I stimulate hope however I can: combing bookstores for inspirational writing, seeking out people who've got pizazz, listening to Mozart and Tina Turner, playing with puppies and polliwogs.

Still, I want more ways to thrive. I've always been conservative, thrifty, economical. "Make-do" was my motto. One day I decided, enough of that! I'm changing my poverty mentality and becoming generous, even to myself. I practice giving for sheer pleasure, indulge myself, and embrace the eccentric, the bizarre, and other people's quirks—everything that's wild as long as it is wonderful, too. I no longer get pulled into the riptide of Dan's criticism. I am emerging. I'm changing from within, while making the most of what I can't control.

> ### *Age may wrinkle the face*
> ### *but lack of enthusiasm wrinkles the soul.*
> ~ Author Unknown

K. I found the ability to adapt and grow goes far beyond those *Be content whatever the circumstances* sermons. I recall the panic and confinement I felt in the beginning as I adjusted to being single-again in an unfamiliar house. Little sun came through the windows. And it wasn't the lack of activity that got me down. After a full day's work, I came home to more: sorting laundry as my printer pounded out the work I had brought home; helping with homework as I proofread. I appreciated friends who helped me regain my sense of self and showed it was possible to make a new start.

I thought of my mother's garden, created with "starts" from friends and relatives. My great-great grandmother tucked a wild yellow rose root in her trunk when she emigrated from Ireland. My mother passed one on to me. "Nurturing a new start takes my mind off myself," she says. "I think about where it came from." Each time a start is given away, it will need to adapt to a new environment and does better if given extra attention.

Friends who were transparent helped me confront my fears; I saw how they had grown through their losses. They helped me accept the divorce card I had been dealt by showing they held different ones that weren't necessarily better: widowhood, illness, problems with children. They gave me confidence I, too, could adapt and thrive on my own again.

Nurturing also came from those who didn't know what to say but stayed in touch anyway. "I apologize," Mary said recently. She and her husband had been our next-door neighbors for over ten years. "I had no idea what you were going through or I would have done things differently." Yet I treasured her telephone calls, invites to tea, and help taping my new answering-machine message. Just remaining my friend was enough.

Arlene had to pursue me. My friend since grade school, she'd been my maid of honor. Embarrassed by the divorce, I seldom stayed in touch, and she couldn't come to the wedding. When we met again after my remarriage, she shared her own troubles. We cried together. I popped open a dusty box of journals and for the first time shared them with another person. Arlene gave me permission to touch my pain again and see it from a distance. The high and low moments I had endured in my crash zone helped her.

> *He comes alongside us*
> *when we go through hard times,*
> *and before you know it,*
> *He brings us alongside someone else*
> *who is going through hard times*
> *so that we can be there for that person*
> *just as God was there for us.*
>
> ⌒ 2 Corinthians 1:3-4, The Message

Friends Are Symbols That Life Goes On

Friends boost your immune system, according to psychologist Blair Justice of the University of Texas-Houston School of Public Health.[2] A landmark study at the University of Michigan revealed that "the lack of supportive relationships is a factor that is almost as dangerous as well-known risks such as smoking, high blood pressure, or obesity."[3] True friends sense the velocity of the wind against your soul, knowing when to encourage or simply say nothing. When your hopes are dashed, friends encourage you to keep your chin up. With true friends, you do more than survive; you supersede circumstances. You believe you can start again. Here's what some divorcing women we know did:

Debbie refused to withdraw. She found a friend to share secrets with—Robbie, who pulled her into the singles group. They started a singles pew in their church.

Jane was afraid nobody would like her if they knew her struggles. After she joined a parents' committee at school, she met Jack and Sharon, who included her in weekend outings.

Carrie invited an elderly friend for donuts and a visit to a garden nursery every other Saturday morning. She says, "The companionship and mutual interest in flowers took away the loneliness."

Katherine didn't have children, but she knew healthy touch heals. She put her name on the calendar: a haircut every five weeks, a facial, manicure, a massage now and then.

When Karen's brother-in-law, Allan, said, "You troubled the marriage so he had to go outside to meet his needs," she started defending herself. Then, realizing Allan had shame issues similar to her ex's, she let it go. When he later accused, "You have never admitted your responsibility…," she responded, "I realize I forced him out because I wouldn't accept his mistress—and failed to meet his needs for large breasts. Don't you get it, Allan?"

Barb's best friend never wanted to marry again; but Barb didn't feel that way. She chose to believe the longings of her heart validated God's will for her. She realized no Mr. Wonderful was going to make everything perfect, but she kept handing her feelings to God and claiming His promises.

June called Linda after every harassing phone call from her ex. Linda was smart enough to say, "I love you. You're going to be all right," every time.

Beth's formerly close friends shut her out but invited her ex and children over for social occasions. Instead of starting a feud, she realized friends like that were not a big loss and found moral support elsewhere.

Kate had always longed for sexy encounters with her husband that never happened; now she wanted a handsome man to come along and rip her clothes off. When Monica told her, "Yeah, what you need is to get laid," Kate thought about it; then her values won out. She knew she had to live with herself.

Kari visited Israel when Melanie spent the first Christmas with her dad. That summer, she met her parents for trout fishing in Colorado during the week her daughter spent at camp. "I needed something to look forward to and interaction with others."

Noelle felt like staying in after the news of Dan and The Neighbor broke in their small town, but she forced herself out to community and school events. "My children's welfare took priority over anybody's perception of me."

The essence of genius
lies in knowing what to overlook.

∽ William James

Wiser in Love

"You are now a one-person couple," author Ingrid Trobisch tells single people she meets. Happily married many years and widowed nearly as long, she affirms singles in her worldwide family ministry, telling them to nurture both the feminine and masculine sides of themselves. Drawing from C.S. Lewis' wisdom, she insists we are all coupled; there's just the difference between the one-person and two-person couples. One doesn't need a life-mate to validate either your existence or your worth.

"Love doesn't mean possession, and company doesn't mean security," says Veronica Shoffstaff in a poignant poem, *After Awhile*. She says joys and sorrows are ever present, even in love.

K: I was carrying a pot of baked beans to a barbeque when I met the man of my dreams. It was an ordinary day. In the months that followed, I danced between afraid-to-trust-again and wanting-to-risk-it. I told the Lord to take this man out of my life if he wasn't right for me.

Shortly before Richard asked me to marry him, he learned of an acoustic neuroma (tumor) behind his left ear. Without surgery his life expectancy was only ten years. Since surgery might leave his face paralyzed, he thought it best to end our romantic involvement.

"If that's what you want," I said as he walked to his car.

Richard turned around. "I know what I want," he said, "and I'm looking at it." That crisis solidified our love. Together, we determined to cope with whatever happened. I addressed wedding invitations in the hospital waiting room while he underwent the risky eight-hour operation. The surgery left him with balance and hearing on the right side only, and an unexplainable nerve-related ringing in the deaf ear. In addition to tolerating this constant internal noise, Richard had to learn to walk, drive, and ride a bicycle all over again.

The two of us held few illusions about riding off into an exquisite sunset. I'm glad, because four days before the wedding, the Loma Prieta earthquake shook the area. Shipments into San Francisco were curtailed, including deliveries of cut flowers. When the lady creating my bouquets shared her dilemma, I said, "Then we'll get a chrysanthemum plant at Safeway and whack off the flowers." When the windows fell out of the hotel we'd booked for our wedding night, and several guests called to say damages would prevent their attendance, we settled for any available hotel room, and we went on with the ceremony.

For me, thriving is picking yourself back up and going on with the ceremony of living. The only time I won't be hanging on for dear life is when I'm dead. Although finding a second love is an enviable position to be in, I know that having a life partner isn't a shield from crash zones.

The best things are the nearest; breath in your nostrils, light in your eyes, flowers at your feet, duties at your hand, the path of God just before you.

⁓ Robert Louis Stevenson

N: "How do you do this single stuff?" I asked a never-married friend. "I'm not getting the hang of it."

"Now you know why I'm so neurotic!" she replied.

I laughed. In spite of what I'm missing, some days I know I'm happier than I've been in years. Statistics show men get married faster after divorce, whereas women tend to adapt better, appreciating the autonomy singleness offers. Even when they didn't want divorce, a whopping 80 percent of women say they are better off afterwards.

I have to admit, part of my joy comes in the potential of meeting a man who also wants to commit to romantic love. I've heard remarried women say, "Now I know how love is supposed to feel." Actress Jane Seymour (TV's Dr. Quinn Medicine Woman) said on a *Oprah* broadcast, "I came out of a very bad situation and didn't know if I would ever know love again. When I did, I realized it was the only love I'd ever known."

Something about these statements touches me. I hope to be wiser in love; I know I am in life. My days may be uneventful but they're filled with more than romantic dreams. My inner life is rich. And there are the real things: kids to raise, flocks to feed, wounded to tend, people to bless—the "I've been there" kind of blessing only I can give. And I think that I'm about to!

For the vision is yet for an appointed time;
But at the end it will speak, and it will not lie.
Though it tarries, wait for it;
Because it will surely come.
It will not tarry.

~ Habakkuk 2:3

Surf's Up

Life in the crash zone is wind whipped and scary. But each surging breaker is like the contractions of childbirth. With each pulse, new life is pushed farther onto the shore like intricate driftwood and beautiful shells in which a multitude of fragile living organisms thrive. Hidden in the crevices is a multitude of micro-life which has adapted to the rush, the roar, and the rhythm. You, too, can live in the crash zone. Though pounded, you won't be crushed. Knocked down, you'll get up. Let enthusiasm and exuberance drive you forward.

Heart Work:

Using indelible ink, write your name on a shell. As you place it on your nightstand, remember that persistence pays. Soon you'll start to thrive.

13

I Like
The New Me

*But we speak the wisdom of God in a mystery,
the hidden wisdom which God ordained . . .*

~ 1 Corinthians 2:7

*A*ll she had to do was enjoy life: A twenty-million-dollar fortune, a thousand dollars a day in royalties. But Sarah could not. This forty-four-year-old widow was afraid of the dead.

Following the death of her husband, William Wirt Winchester (the rifle king's son), in Hartford, Connecticut, Sarah consulted a spirit medium in Boston. Séances confirmed her fears—the Winchester Rifle fortune was haunted by the ghosts of millions of Indians, settlers, and animals killed by the "repeater" rifles that won the West! Messages from the spirit world insisted that Sarah make her surroundings appeal to first-class spooks who would confuse and keep the evil ones away. "Get a larger house," the spiritist advised. "Fix it up however the spirits require."

So Sarah Pardee Winchester crossed the Continental Divide and bought an eighteen-room house on six acres south of San Francisco. For the next thirty-eight years, carpenters worked twenty-four hours a day as she pored over building books. Sitting in the séance room at the heart of her house, Sarah devised bizarre plans for remodeling and enlarging what is now known as the Winchester Mystery House in San Jose, California. She did not live to build but incessantly built to live.

The puzzled workers did not know that the Boston medium had promised nothing bad would happen to Sarah as long as hammers rang. Workers were hired and fired. "Build switchback stairs here; two-inch risers there," they were told. "Tear down that column; rebuild it upside down." The house became a 160-room mansion overlooking lavish gardens and a view of the Santa Clara Valley beyond. The mansion had forty-six fireplaces, thirteen bathrooms, three elevators, rooms with rare scalloped French Lincresta wall coverings. It rose seven stories until the 1906 earth-quake reduced its highest point to a fourth-floor balcony. Whatever the spirits wanted, the spirits got, including a priceless Tiffany window installed on an inside wall where daylight never reveals the multicolored radiance for which it was created.

The hallway to the center of the home is like a maze. A stair-way leads to a wall with no door. Several doors open to solid walls. Lighting is arranged so no shadows are cast. Windows have thirteen panes; walls, thirteen panels; chandeliers, thirteen globes; and the greenhouse, thirteen cupolas. At Sarah's request, a bell tolled at midnight, one A.M., and two A.M., as a signal for spirits to scurry back to their graves.

Mrs. Winchester refused to be photographed. Only her Chinese butler was permitted to see her face. After an earthquake trapped her in a front bedroom, Sarah sealed off that part of the house, allowing no one entrance through the front door, includ-ing then-President Teddy Roosevelt.

At her death in 1922, only four million dollars remained of the fortune. Her rambling home remains unfinished, a brooding reminder of a reclusive, fear-driven woman. Although she lived in a richly furnished house full of French beveled-glass mirrors, fifty-two skylights, and more than ten thousand windows, Sarah Pardee Winchester was controlled by darkness.[1]

The worst evil of all
is to leave the ranks of the living before one dies.

～ Seneca

A Fabulous Fortune

Divorce vests you with a legacy of destruction, but inherent in that legacy is the opportunity to acquire holy wisdom. With your divorce, you crossed a dividing line; you'll never live the way you did before. Wisdom shatters illusions, opens doors, dispels darkness by letting in light. You need no longer hunker down, wounded, silent, walled in a warped reality. You are not a frumpy farmhouse; God intends you to be a richly furnished mansion.

Your eternal spirit houses awesome things prepared by a loving God whose Holy Spirit is leading you into all truth. You now touch the hidden things, but not through magic or a medium.

Under the leadership of Jesus Christ, you are illuminated and enlightened as you traverse the maze of divorce. The use of the word *mase* dates back to thirteenth-century Chaucer. It represents, in the face of many obstacles like deception, delusion, and disappointment, a journey to seek the center of truth.

> *You thought you were going to be made*
> *into a decent little cottage?*
> *He is building a palace.*
> *And He intends to come and live in it Himself.*
>
> ~ C.S. Lewis

Inherent in divorce is an opportunity to possess the priceless wisdom of discernment (a clear mind) and insight (the ability to see with your spirit).

TO DISCERN: to perceive by the sight or other sense or by the intellect; to distinguish mentally.

INSIGHT: an instance of apprehending the true nature of a thing through intuitive understanding.[2]

Priceless wisdom makes you savvy. An internal light bulb clicks on allowing you to see more than you saw before (Luke 11:34-36). What you discover is not what you expect—you can now put your finger on subtle discrepancies. You can begin to identify irrational thinking as it occurs, and you can confront it. You can begin to see through manipulation and the emotional control that may have been used against you in the past. You connect with your own integrity.

"O LORD, who may abide in Thy tent?" asked the psalmist (Ps. 15:1, NASB). The answer: "He who walks with integrity, and works righteousness, and speaks truth in his heart" (vs. 2). Integrity is the sum of the equation when you combine discernment with insight. Random House *Webster's* defines *integrity* as "uncompromising adherence to moral and ethical principles, soundness of moral character; honesty; the state of being whole or entire."[3] God's desire for you is this state of being whole, the reintegration (or integrity) of your soul, spirit, and body after its fragmentation in divorce. His principles work: You are wise to rely on what you know is true and on the One you know is the Truth (John 14:6).

As your integrity is confirmed, your femininity is affirmed. It shows in the way you carry yourself. Walking through the maze, and sticking with your aspiration for a better life, you can acquire an air of reverence and grace that make you charming and interesting. What you are going through will add to your mystique. You wear strength and dignity well (Prov. 31:25). People are attracted by what you stand for: innocence, purity, and a tender heart. As you follow God, ingest His Word, and refuse to be sidetracked by pain or the possible wiles of your ex, wisdom validates all the changes that are making you someone new.

Purity of heart is to will one thing.

∼ Soren Kierkegaard

N: When Dan left, the last thing he said was, "I'm not going to be depressed anymore." The last thing I said was, "You will take your depression with you."

I kept trying to figure things out, linking clues, piecing together fragments of knowledge, always hoping Dan would change his mind. When he didn't, I tried to change. When I didn't progress, he ridiculed my efforts. When I did progress, he kept saying, "You just don't get it." But I *was* beginning to get it—he knew it, and it scared him.

His only defense was projected guilt and distorting the truth. The ultimate betrayal is that Dan knowingly trampled on what was most important to me: purity of mind and body, integrity, and character. Creating sympathy for himself, he twisted the reason behind our breakup to justify his leaving. I don't blame anyone who may have believed him; after all, I believed him for twenty years. But these are abuses at the deepest level because the losses can never be validated.

Today my ravaged heart and mind are healing; he can never rob me of a clear conscience. When I look into Dan's eyes, I know he knows the truth.

God's gift of deeper insight made me aware of the big picture and continues to illuminate my thinking. I have come so far that I am not afraid of facing the worst. I have "been there, done that," and it set me free.

It is not easy living, worshiping, and working as a divorced woman in the Christian community. You realize that in the eyes of many, your reputation is sullied. There are always those who will distrust your spirituality. But it is enough to place yourself in the light of God. No matter the brutalizing of your sexuality or femininity, no one on earth can touch your purity of heart.

Wake up! Wisdom says. The answers are all around you.

Proverbs 1:20

"Cry out for her [wisdom]... seek... search...find the knowledge of God."

Proverbs 2:2-5

The Principal Thing

The holy wisdom of discernment and insight has nothing to do with the occult, a pathetic copy of the Creator's mystery. The occult is a counterfeit that twists evil into good, darkness into light, or bitter into sweet (Isa. 5:20). Scripture says wisdom is the principal thing, more precious than rubies (Prov. 3:15). Its acquisition is better than pearls (Job 28:18). Wisdom leads the way as you perceive what you otherwise could not and you understand what otherwise is enigma or riddle (Prov. 1:1-6).

Divorce exposes who you are in a way that marriage never did. At first, you build walls for protection. But walls also keep out the good. Asking God for His wisdom will keep you installing windows that allow fresh insights and new possibilities to flow through. Disgrace is replaced with grace; your lost dignity, with glory.

"Our spiritual and emotional growth is God's 'interest' on his investment in us," say authors Henry Cloud and John Townsend. When divorce traps you in a confusing maze, wisdom leads you out. It guards the door, helping you establish healthy boundaries. It teaches whom to let inside, how to say "no," and when to know the difference. According to Cloud and Townsend, "When we say 'no' to people and activities that are hurtful to us, we are protecting God's investment."[4]

A woman of insight knows who she is and does not apologize for her identity. She is like the colors of dawn pouring through a priceless Tiffany window: Reflective. Beautiful. Her life is like a grand Victorian door welcoming her household and visitors from everywhere: Gracious. Solid. Sound.

> She who knows not, and knows not that she knows not, is a fool; shun her;
> She who knows not, and knows that she knows not, is a child; teach her.
> She who knows, and knows not that she knows, is asleep; wake her;

She who knows, and knows that she knows, is wise; follow her.

Author Unknown

...That the eyes of your heart may be enlightened
in order that you may know the hope
to which he has called you,
the riches of his glorious inheritance
in the saints, and his incomparably great power
for us who believe...

∼ Ephesians 1:18-19, NIV

Wise Women of Discernment

As divorced people, we are not a tribe unto ourselves. Like every other human being, we like and need to be with couples. We enjoy the companionship of both old and young adults and the company of children. We often miss masculine dialogue. We have something to give as well as receive. The body of Christ needs us as much as we need the body. Isolation in singles or midlife groups is not a healthy option.

Divorce does not mean you have been placed in God's basement. Withdrawing, whether self-imposed through fear, as in Sarah's case, or imposed by the expectations of others and culture, is not worthy of you. To identify only with biblical characters whose suffering parallels your own stifles growth. You need to expand your horizons now. Look at the women who, with or without a man, took a stand and changed things.

Achsah was the daughter of Caleb, one of the original spies into the Promised Land. When her husband was not man enough to request a worthy inheritance, she did!

"Give me a blessing," she asked her father, acting from an inner sense of what was appropriate, though beyond what was customary or traditional. "Since you have given me land...give me also springs of water" (Josh. 15:19).

Isn't that the cry of your heart, too? Your birthright is not only a piece of land, but springs that help you supply your family's needs and replenish your own emotional/spiritual cisterns. But it seems like "springs" don't always come with the territory. There are times when you need to boldly ask, reverencing your own worthiness in the community, in the church, and as a child of God.

The story of another bold lady, the prophetess and judge Deborah, is related in Judges 4. Day after day, Deborah watched what twenty years of oppression were doing to her people. She grew tired of the harassment. Her example teaches that courage, faith, and love for God result in excellent consequences not only for ourselves, but for the people with whom we belong.

"Hasn't God promised to deliver the enemy into our hands, nine hundred iron chariots and all?" she asked a man named Barak. But it seemed no one had guts to stand against the intimidation.

"If you go with me, then I will go," Barak said, "but if you will not go with me, I will not go" (Jud. 4:8).

Barak underestimated Deborah.

"Guess what? I *am* going!" she said. "But there'll be no glory for you! God will sell Sisera into the hand of a woman!" Deborah wasn't talking about personal glory; final victory came when a woman named Jael pegged Commander Sisera and went down in history, too. Grounded in hidden wisdom, Deborah picked up on what God wanted and went for it! And Israel defeated Jabin, king of Canaan.

"Awake, awake, Deborah! Awake, awake, sing a song!" Barak and Deborah sang as praise to God (Jud. 5:12). "Let those who love Him be like the sun when it comes out in full strength" (vs. 31). Her story ends with this phrase: "So the land had rest for forty years" (vs. 31).

Deborah lived in a state of grace. Her discernment brought freedom to her people. Her wakefulness radiated strength.

The sunlight is your inheritance, too. There may be no direct example of divorced women in the Bible, but that does not mean it has nothing specific to say to you. Perhaps God, respecting your personhood and dignity, regardless of your marital state, is including you in the larger picture, rather than categorizing you, as people are wont to do. Like married women, or the never-married, young, old, and all ages in between, you, too, can read these passages for inspiration about how God desires to bless you as a citizen of His kingdom. Discover how He plans to use your life to continue to bless others.

> *Not to speak out against evil is to ignore the truth.*
>
> ∿ Dr. Anthony Fortosis

K: "I walked away from the woman God gave me," Ed said the day our divorce was final.

Though armed with textbook knowledge of midlife crisis and childhood trauma, and a few sketchy hunches, I never could justify his decision to leave his family. I'm still uncovering clues I had ignored. I may never fully know, nor do I need to.

I was raised to place my trust in parents, pastors, teachers, husband. I counted on their honesty. I had learned love is not suspicious. But dishonest people say and do exactly what it takes to overcome doubts. Ed was a master at quelling my quest for truth.

Once I telephoned him with news of a possible tumor on a mammogram and the doctor's request for repeat films. Trying to reconcile his vague response with what I'd hoped he'd say, I asked, "If this is cancer, you won't be here for me, will you?"

He said that he would have to think about it.

I was paralyzed between knowing something was wrong and wanting not to know.

Another time I asked Ed to be honest about what was bothering him. He turned defensive. "Be open with me," I tried again.

He told me he was dealing with me now and how to keep me happy.

My question was on target the first time; his response was phrased to get me off track.

Even Ed's tone of voice and body language was calculated to throw me off balance. I remember my anguish over how his lifestyle of arriving home late, then leaving at three in the morning, confused our daughter in the final days before he vacated the family home. One night before I went to bed I taped a brief note to his lounge chair suggesting he move out while we waited for the house to sell. He stormed into the bedroom after midnight cursing that I couldn't do anything about it and challenging me to kick him out.

Until it happened to me, I never understood why some women stay in crazy-making relationships. To gain insight into my confusing maze, I investigated the roles in which I had been cast: Ed's surrogate mother, caretaker, and business partner; the wrong-doer; and the crazy one. And I woke up. Divorce taught me to pay attention to what I value. I am not afraid to question answers. Today I know that a man who answers his wife the way Ed so often did me, squashing conversations, has serious identity issues. His harassing letters are not worth the postage stamp to respond. Today his responses would be unacceptable. I recognize his diversion tactics; he doesn't get away with them. Instead of an assault on my worth, I perceive they expose his own heart.

If my mind says one thing and spirit another, I ask myself, "What's wrong here?" I protect what's important to me, such as a peaceful house without put-downs. Now I shudder at Melanie's recall of Ed's remark to her: "You only have to put up with your mother until you're eighteen; then you get the heck out." At the time fear left me speechless. Now there's no more scurrying under cover because I'm afraid to speak up. No longer do I wait for someday to get on with my life.

Since Ed walked away, I am a much wiser woman.

The less you think of yourself,
the more you give of yourself too freely—
and the less you have left to live on.

∽ Art Ciancio

You Are Not a Frumpy Farmhouse

Too often women guard a happy-marriage image and cover up bruises from abuse, control, and relationship manipulation. Perhaps the messages started early in childhood with, "Act like a lady. Don't talk back. Good girls don't..." Later, they evolved into, "You're trying to make me look bad. You provoke me. I did it because of you." After divorce, the messages continued with, "Keep your dirty laundry to yourself. Try to understand he means well. It wasn't that bad; you can't prove it. You're not perfect. You enabled him. Quit whining."

These messages can throw you off balance. Spirit bruising discolors your reality and warps the truth. When someone else says what you felt, saw, or said is not what happened, you "disintegrate." Your integrity has been "d-i-s'ed," or invalidated. Unable to reconcile what's happening within you with what is going on out there, you doubt yourself.

Did you keep hurts a secret? seal off part of your heart? use up energy dodging verbal bullets or lugging his emotional baggage or ammunition? "There are two losses here to recognize," says Patricia Evans, author of *The Verbally Abusive Relationship*. They are loss of love and loss of self.

"If we were in the hands of an enemy we would know there was little or no truth in what we heard," says Evans. However a wife doesn't always "know she is being opposed for the sake of opposing." The integrity of your foundation as an infinitely valuable person has been assaulted if you were deceived, your feelings trivialized, or things confided in privacy were twisted and used to put you down. "Learning to doubt yourself and believe something is wrong with you are all symptoms of shattered integrity," says Evans. If a verbally abusing mate was a church leader or community pillar, the resulting confusion is doubly humiliating.[5]

Spirit and soul bruising does not necessarily cease with a divorce decree or restraining order. Manipulation does not scurry off to a grave. You need distance to give discernment and insight a fighting chance to free your spirit. Perhaps for the first time you now see that when you let down your hair in the safety of your home, you made yourself vulnerable. Vulnerability and trust are appropriate within marriage. If he used these to take advantage of you, or they were turned against you, it is not a reflection on your integrity. Do not wound the new woman emerging by being sorry that you trusted. You no longer need to tiptoe around your own heart.

We carry with us the wonders we seek without us.

⁓ Sir Thomas Browne

Employ Insight to Shore Up Your Boundaries

Reconstructing your perception of out-of-control situations begins when you respect your gift of discernment and your gift of insight. The gift here is an inner knowing that *you know* that you know that you know, even when you have no concrete evidence. Like the flaky Greek pastry baklava made from layers of phyllo dough, you have layer upon layer of paper-thin suspicions that have accumulated through the years. Your spirit is saying, *The uneasiness is building. There's something here to which I need to pay attention.*

This is not New Age hocus-pocus but a God-given tool to preserve and protect you and the things important to you: your thoughts, values, desires, and needs; the ability to give and receive love; and even your skin (if you've been physically battered, you know what we mean).

When you are violated by a manipulator/abuser, your initial temptation is to explain it away. *I must have imagined this*, you tell yourself. *It isn't that bad.* But the uneasiness does not dissipate. You fear abandonment and don't want to admit it. Your spirit is seeking to level the unsettling experience. Someone you loved, and thought loved you, twisted both what you did or said and what you didn't do. You chalk it up to fatigue, stress, midlife crisis, or the devil. But beneath awareness, you know, *Something is wrong with this picture.*

Jeff Klippenes, ordained minister and marriage-family-child counselor, freely uses the word *intuition* to refer to this gift of communication and says, "I believe it is left over from the Garden of Eden. Man and woman were transparent, knowing each other completely on a deeper level than the verbal or physical."

"We need to honor the remnant of our intuition," claims Klippenes, "not run from it."[6]

Intuition is a controversial word in the Christian community. Is it because we are afraid of it, the way Adam and Eve were when they knew that they were naked (Gen. 3:7-8)? Intuition disrobes mysteries and reveals things as they are. But in the context of sin, it scares us, makes us hide. Looking back at the garden we see how Satan cunningly confused Eve's clarity of mind and discounted her insight about God's will by telling a lie concealed in a truth (Gen. 3:2-5). The father of lies (John 8:44) invalidated what she knew to be true: that God had one restriction required for residency in Eden (Gen 2:17). Eve lost her integrity (wholeness) the day she and her mate ate the fruit of the tree of the knowledge of good and evil (Gen. 3:2-6). Since then all humanity lives under the shadow of death (Ps. 23:4). Since then we see "through a glass darkly" (1 Cor. 13:12, KJV).

Insight and discernment, or the intuition Klippenes refers to, may be the *things* Paul refers to in 1 Corinthians 2:13-14 as "comparing spiritual things with spiritual." He previously describes God's wisdom as "hidden," spoken in a "mystery," saying, "God has revealed them to us through His Spirit. For the Spirit searches all things, yes, the deep things of God....that we might know the things that have been freely given to us by God" (1 Cor. 2:10, 12). You do not need to fully understand why you are feeling what you are feeling to put deeper insight to work performing reality checks.

The writer of Proverbs wrote, "Trust in the LORD with all your heart and lean not on your own understanding" (Prov. 3:5). He was aware that relying on your mental faculties alone is not enough in this hazy world. You are to trust in Someone Higher whose spirit, like yours, will not fit within the small box of your own understanding.

"Women are called by God to be mothers, to nurture and are given intuition and discernment that most men do not have," says Rev. Jerry Falwell.[7] We often leave deeper insight/intuition on the shelf of our experience to gather dust because we can't scientifically prove or spiritually explain it to ourselves or others. But that does not mean truth cannot be discerned.

The Spirit of God leads you into truth (John 16:13) when you are ready to receive it. The story about Jesus walking on water records that the disciples "were greatly astonished" (Mk. 6:51, NASB) when Jesus climbed in the boat with them. Why? Because "they had not gained any insight from the incident of the loaves, but their heart was hardened" (6:52, NASB). We may not be in a position to handle learning the truth that insight brings even though Scripture says "a man will be praised according to his insight" (Prov. 12:8, NASB). Solomon, the wisest man, discovered, "in much wisdom there is much grief, and increasing knowledge results in increasing pain" (Ecc. 1:18, NASB). Sometimes we don't want to know the truth. God may wait until we are ready and able to handle it.

Wisdom is God's delight (Prov. 8:30). It begins when we fear Him, says the psalmist (Ps. 111:10). But to get there, most of us

take the circuitous route through the maze of our own understanding. Wanting quick answers and solutions, we forget that
knowing Him is a process. Can we fully understand what He is
doing, when, or why? The *Living Bible* paraphrase of 1
Corinthians 2:14-16 puts it this way:

. . . "Only those who have the Holy Spirit within them can
understand what the Holy Spirit means. Others just can't take it
in. But the spiritual man has insight into everything, and that
bothers and baffles the man of the world, who can't understand
him at all. How could he? For certainly he has never been one to
know the Lord's thoughts, or to discuss them with him, or to
move the hands of God by prayer. But strange as it seems, we
Christians actually do have within us a portion of the very
thoughts and mind of Christ."

God wants access in order to free you from the intimidation
you feel in the presence of a controller. Throw open the sashes
and bat your eyelashes. Pick up on nuances in the other person's
innuendos. Hear every word he doesn't say. Listen for the "Ah-ha"
in your spirit. Here's help:

1. *Cut yourself some slack.*

Manipulation and abuse are cumulative. Each encounter with
a controller tilts you further off your rocker, an integral part of
that person's agenda. Led into a maze of helplessness where you
can't explain why you feel upset (angry, confused, hysterical,
depressed) or act out (yell, cry, slam cupboards, throw things) you
can't decipher what is happening or connect past incidents to
today's. Find a quiet place. Take a deep breath.

2. *Welcome your rising annoyance, that off-balance sensation.*

It is there as a warning. Wake up to signals in your body
language; you stiffen or slump, you clench your jaw. Notice how
fear places manipulators in control; they count on emotional
shock waves that leave you reeling.

3. *Watch for attack-and-evasion techniques.*

Manipulators are skilled at their agenda. They tap your soft spots, including your fear of hurting another's feelings. They motivate by projecting false guilt that you can do more; so when you drop your guard, you will nurse their wounds or handle their responsibilities. They listen for your vulnerabilities, then use them to stab you later.

4. *Just say "no."*

Catch your initial defensive reaction to say too much or not enough. Decide for a neutral, non-threatening environment. Simply walk away. If you stay and things get out of hand, say, "I refuse to be treated like that." You can choose where you want to live emotionally.

5. *Accept the risks.*

Waking up to the truth doesn't mean others will change or stick around; manipulators will abandon you if they don't get their way. Expect it. "Sometimes setting boundaries clarifies that you were left a long time ago, in every way perhaps, except physically," says John Townsend. "Boundaries are a 'litmus test' for the qualities of our relationships. Those who can't respect our boundaries are telling us that they don't love our 'No.' They only love our 'Yes,' our compliance."[8]

6. *Consider this remodeling tip from Sarah Winchester's life:*

Never let fear seal off your inner house; it also shuts out the light. History is a credible teacher. Let past manipulative/abusive experiences reveal your need to intuit in future relationships. As you boldly step across the threshold toward a new you, in time you will learn again to trust yourself, God, and trustworthy others.

I have come back again to where I belong;
not an enchanted place, but the walls are strong.

～ Dorothy H. Rath

K • For too long I abdicated my good sense. Divorce helped
me see I had allowed Ed to take away parts of myself
that God values. I'd been taught to please, often apologizing
simply to avoid conflict. "I'm a different person now," I told my
mother. "You may not like what you hear coming out of my
mouth." I'm not sure she understood that I'm discovering a
person I never allowed myself to be.

I'm still gullible at times—sometimes denial appears the easi-
est route—but I'm making progress. I enrolled in a management
class on dealing with difficult people and began to understand
that deferring to another's wishes isn't necessarily an act of love.
Saying "no" to a coworker or boss, a church committee or someone significant in my life doesn't mean I'm not honoring God.

I'm getting over the criticism leveled at me that I'm self-absorbed
if I draw a line or if I walk away and refuse to engage with toxic
people. Never again do I want to lose myself because I fear speaking up. No more whitewashing demeaning remarks disguised as
jokes. Living free from fear of what others think, being able to trust,
and honoring my pure heart are important to me. I need people in
my life who allow me to do that, who value my independent
thoughts, appreciate my talents, and encourage the hopes and
respect the desires God placed in my heart. I conserve my
emotional energy to bless the world, not just pacify at any price.

Eye has not seen, nor ear heard,
Nor have entered into the heart of man
The things which God has prepared
for those who love him.

～ 1 Corinthians 2:9

It takes two to tangle: one vulnerable person and another who exploits through inappropriate use of emotional power. A manipulator locates vulnerability by trial and error then uses that knowledge to distress and bring pressure to bear. Protect your tender heart. Because you don't easily recognize when you are being overpowered, awareness of your vulnerable spots is imperative.

- *Your feelings are discounted and undermined:*

  When he says, *"You make a big deal out of nothing, can't take a joke, always complain, take things too seriously, jump to conclusions, blow it out of proportion,"* **you feel** *insecure, confused, invalidated; you fear disapproval, want to appease and/or conform. His intention is to insinuate your feelings are bad, instead of neutral and worth talking about.*

You Are a Mansion

Wisdom teaches that what you came to believe were your failings are in actuality your gifts. Now you recognize things as they really are. When you tolerated more, committed to loving in spite of pain, and retreated to keep the peace, your partner perceived it as weakness and used it to his advantage. Your perceptions were not validated. Part of the recovery of the spirit is realizing what was going on under the surface.

For example, if you never felt accepted by your mate, a legitimate human need was not being met. It is a valid loss. Spiritual recovery and nourishment comes as your spirit validates your needs, rights, and losses. Discernment is the conscious acknowledgment of what your spirit already knows. When you integrate the loss into your life experience, you obtain wisdom. Each step takes you to the next. You lost love, but you did not lose yourself—permanently. Your self-esteem can be torn down, but never your self-worth.

From now on, refuse to leave your spirit unguarded. Let no one trample your perceptions or discount your feelings. Clutch the sword of the Spirit: truth. You have a purpose to accomplish and need your wits about you to complete what God said He will finish in and through you.

You are not asked to lose yourself to the extent that you have nothing left to live on. Biblical submission is not about someone else controlling you in Jesus' name. Both women and men, living in the same household of faith as children of the King, are called to serve the other (Gal. 5:13). An escape clause was not drawn up for either gender. Get to know exploitation techniques that discount, divert, and deny your reality (see sidebar).

N: Truth always surfaces. As I kept listening to my spirit, seeking insight, three instances of dramatic revelation brought my understanding of what was really happening to a climax. I do not know why the Holy Spirit chose to reveal what He did when He did— once through a dream and twice through supernatural knowledge. I had no evidence, no way of knowing about the longterm double life of my spouse at that time. Only after I confronted Dan, did he acknowledge and confirm the facts.

> **Behold, I send you out as sheep in the midst of wolves.**
> **Therefore be wise as serpents and harmless as doves.**
>
> ~ Matthew 10:16

Initially, they were mind-boggling, horrendously painful. I'm glad now that my eyes were enlightened. Instead of forever blaming myself, I saw clearly why I kept hitting walls in prayer and got nowhere in my desire to renew intimacy and rejuvenate our marriage. God cannot change another person's will. When light exposed the bigger picture, I was able to disconnect emotionally from Dan and move forward. No amount of pleading would

* *You are diverted from the real issues:*

  When he says, *"Just drop it, get off my back, give me space, chill out. You heard me, know what I meant, always have to be right,"* **you are** *getting too close to the truth; he can't afford to face it or feel his feelings, fears conflict and anger, makes himself the victim.*

* *You are blamed and criticized:*

  When he says, *"You're looking for trouble, always take the last word, are never satisfied, have expectations that are too big, wouldn't understand, don't get it, think you're so smart,"* **you feel** *irrationally guilty, in denial, selfish, traumatized by nagging; he knows exactly how much resistance will be offered before you break down.*

* *You are controlled by silence, withdrawal, forgetting:*

  When he says, *"Whatever you say dear, it'll be all right, wait and see, I don't have to listen to this, you're making that up, you heard me wrong, I have to go..."* *(door slams),* **you feel** *worn down by his absence, played against someone else, at a dead end, given no option but to protest in nonverbal ways; he then uses those to invalidate, blame and divert you in an ongoing cycle: "you make a big deal out of nothing..."*

What You Can Do

• *Maintain objectivity. Don't allow anyone to make you assume things that are not true.*

• *Define things he says that arouse feelings of power-lessness and confusion. Use them as cues to be cautious and wary.*

• *Process flashbacks, because when you recognize your vulnerable spots and what was used against you, you gain insight.*

• *Be alert when he plays the blame and shame game. You don't have to defend yourself or dignify his critique with a response.*

• *If you feel uncomfortable with any comment, it is a red flag to walk away.*

change anything if he chose not to address the issues. Now I realize that where deception, addiction, and manipulation are at work, human knowledge does not suffice.

When Dan and The Neighbor broke up, he used the news as an opportunity to apologize for hurting me. But inconsistencies in his story were warning lights. Later, my discovery that even those details were couched in lies confirmed what had taken me so long to figure out. The breach of trust was complete. That's when I felt God saying, "Follow Me, and let the dead bury their own dead" (Matt. 8:22).

I want to be an open window, to let light put out the darkness, to discern more than before in ongoing communication with Dan. To hear the difference between what is real and what is phony, especially in the Christian community. I want what happened to me to be part of what God uses to help others.

*The God of our Lord Jesus Christ,
the Father of Glory...
give to you the spirit
of wisdom and revelation
in the knowledge of Him,
the eyes of your understanding
being enlightened . . .*

~ Ephesians 1:17-18

A Woman with Many Facets

Esther was a gorgeous Tiffany window. She was the embodiment of mystique, which is, according to *Merriam-Webster's*, "an air or attitude of mystery or reverence developing around something or someone."[9] Through her life, light spilled upon straw floors of a peasant's hut and the rare wall coverings and richly carpeted floors of the royal palace. Scripture says she obtained favor with everyone who saw her. In those days, more than ever, a woman's face was her fortune. But Esther knew sex appeal is not an external look but is expressed from the inside out. She won the Queen of Persia beauty contest without requesting special favors (Es. 2:12). Her passion for life was her greatest asset. It led to her destiny: the opportunity to save her Jewish race and culture.

Esther knew who she was and where she'd come from, and she kept her identity intact in a foreign land. She was discerning and insightful—a woman who didn't display all her cards at one time. She allowed mystique to be the trump card.

Esther did not hurry. She built in time. To paraphrase a Kenny Rogers song, "she knew when to hold 'em, knew when to fold 'em." When told she had to appeal to her husband to spare her people, at first she wanted to refuse the assignment. Though she was married to the king, she was well aware that approaching his throne without an invitation meant death. But finally she realized the Jews' safety was worth any price. "If I perish, I perish!" she said (Es. 4:16). Commanding her people to pray diligently, she pondered how to win the king's attention, first by exchanging her fasting clothes for fancy royal robes. When the king welcomed her into his presence, she boldly invited him for dinner without saying why. At the banquet, she changed her mind about telling him yet. "Come again tomorrow," she said. Esther was cooking up courage, or perhaps building his interest by inviting him more than one night.

Esther was complex. Her life held many paradoxes: poverty and riches, duty and glory, fear and courage. She balanced these and let her full humanity shine through. Being multifaceted is about recognizing how far you've come, celebrating your gifts and paradoxes, and living up to your potential in the kingdom.

Like Esther, you, too, can allow mystique to be the trump card in both perilous and predictable situations. How you view what happens to you in life determines what you reflect to others. Mystique is an attitude you choose to convey, like aging gracefully or dying with dignity. It's the same with divorce. You can go through it reluctantly, sheepishly, or with grace. How you do it becomes your style. Maybe it's as elusive as a twinkle in your eye, a knowing nod of the head, a smile. Or it shows in your tone of voice, the thrust of your jaw, the drop of your shoulders. Mystique displays the way you personally relate to your circumstances. Reverence for yourself and for what has happened to you means you respect the refining process of life's losses with a curtsy.

"Mystique can be learned," said women's issues expert, Jean Lush, author of *The Emotional Phases of a Woman's Life*, "often with great effort, but it's not that some are born with it and some are not."[10] This air of reverence about you cannot be defined or formulated, just as God's character cannot be defined. As soon as you try to explain it or list ten easy steps to get it, it's not there anymore. Why do some women seem to have more of it than others? We don't know. It is a quality that defies our ability to categorize. Similar to fragrance, it goes where you go and leaves the lingering scent in the air of who you are and what you've been through. It is like taking your own bouquet of garden-picked roses to the deli for lunch. A room that before smelled like dill pickles is now filled with a fragrant essence. People notice. Mystique is like that. You can carry ambience with you and are not dependent on others to create it or provide it. The mystique of roses and yourself is that thorns are inherent, the difficulties are part of your value now, part of what make you whole, integral, enhancing the world.

Isabella Rossellini says, "There is some unknown force that makes us move all together in one direction or another, toward a given style. It's a fascinating mystery."[11] Perhaps this mystery of reverence is a remnant of being created in the image of God; that of His sweet presence in our earthy, sometimes paltry, lives. As such, it is your birthright as a woman and child of God. Like Esther, you are a window. Through your life God wants to spill light into the mystery of circumstance. You, too, are in a scary place. But you are heading toward your destiny, a new place and a new time. A new you.

> *Here I am! I stand at the door and knock.*
> *If you hear my voice and open the door,*
> *I will come in and eat with you*
> *and you will eat with me.*
>
> ∽ Revelation 3:20

His Threshold

In divorce, as in Sarah Winchester's house, there are many doors. You want to open them but sometimes are timid or afraid. What will you find? Deeper insight? An air of reverence about you that you never knew you had? Increased authenticity? Finely tuned discernment? When will God next do something incredible in and through you? Soon you see He's at the door. Sooner or later you'll find He is the door (John 10:7). Boldly step across the threshold. It's time to say, "Look out, world! I like the new me."

> *Sing, O childless woman!*
> *Break out into loud and joyful song...*
> *for she who was abandoned has more blessings now*
> *than she whose husband stayed!*
> *Enlarge your house;*
> *build on additions;*
> *spread out your home!*
> *For you will soon be bursting at the seams!*
> *...Fear not; you will no longer live in shame.*
> *...For your Creator will be your "husband."*
> *...For the Lord has called you back from your grief—*
> *a young wife abandoned by her husband.*

> ∽ Isaiah 54:1-6, TLB

*H*eart *W*ork:

Start anew. Now is the time to:
. try tofu
. pierce your ears
. plant turnips
. go on a blind date with a bachelor fire chief
. go back to college

Remember Luci Baines Johnson? The daughter of former President Lyndon Johnson dropped out of college to marry and then raised four children. After a divorce and remarriage, she promised herself by age fifty she'd have a university degree. "It was time to finish unfinished business," she says. In 1997, the year her son Lyndon graduated from law school, she earned her diploma, with sixty-nine credits given for "life experience."[12]

Think sideways!

∼ Edward de Bono

14

My Children Are Listening

"I will watch over them to build and to plant,"
says the LORD.
"In those days they shall say no more:
'The fathers have eaten sour grapes,
and the children's teeth are set on edge.'"

∼ Jeremiah 31:28-29

N: I dislike roller coasters. But Space Mountain loomed like a personal challenge in my own Tomorrowland. I'd taken my daughters to Disneyland for the Christmas holidays just weeks after Dan announced his intention to leave. Throughout Frontierland and Fantasyland, I tried hard not to lose it, but the pain of why we were doing this was getting to me. In Tomorrowland, I forced back tears as we moseyed through each labyrinth while waiting our turn at the rides. Finally, the line led into a huge, dark cavern. We couldn't see each other's faces. How I welcomed a place to finally let my tears spill, my sniffling covered by the rattle and rumble of machinery and distant screams.

As the girls and I climbed aboard our spaceship, I noticed a sign warned danger for pregnant women and people with heart conditions. *The rougher the better*, I thought. *Maybe I'll miscarry this terrible trauma.*

Then, off we went, picking up speed. Each turn and twist came as a surprise, because the entire ride was taking place in blackout-simulated outer space. As the ship careened around the first deep curve, a sickening fear rose in my gut.

Pay attention, something told me. I heard clearly formed sentences: *You are going to feel completely out of control. This is a metaphor for your life right now. Don't be afraid. Go with each bump and jolt. Lean into the rolls and rushes. Don't resist. God is with you.*

It was rough. It was tough. But the scariest part of that ride was getting out, jostled and windblown, into the glare of reality. I knew the ride of my life had just begun.

So take a new grip with your tired hands,
stand firm on your shaky legs.

∽ Hebrews 12:12, TLB

The Mother of All Rides

Hop aboard! Single-parenting while recovering from the derailment of a long-term marriage is the mother of all roller-coaster rides. But you can do it. It starts when you're newly divorced, financially challenged, and scared to death. At the same time, you do any or all of these: work full-time, job hunt, taxi your child to school events, attend parent-teacher conferences, help with homework, research day-care, do the bills, clean house, wash laundry, volunteer for field trips, teach Sunday School, and try to find time for a bath. All the while handling your own grief.

Are you at the end of your rope? Yes. Alone? No. In our country, every year 1.2 million single-parent families result from a divorce. Women head most one-parent homes.[1] Since the 1960s the percentage of children living apart from their biological fathers roughly doubled to 36 percent. By the turn of the century nearly 50 percent of American children may be going to sleep each evening without being able to say good-night to their dads.[2]

Sometimes the more you know, the scarier it gets. Other times darkness acts as a cover to keep you from anticipating each jolt in the journey. You'll twist and turn through guilt, mistakes, and humiliation. Take each curve as it comes: Your children testing you (they may appear resilient but have a pocketful of resentment—or the opposite). Your ex-spouse outwitting you (he may undermine your authority). The other woman taunting you (she may threaten your position as role model). Relatives or friends misunderstanding you (they may offer hurtful advice).

Lean into the turns. Expect the unexpected. Prepare for the unpredictable. You are a remarkable human being with a desire to do the best you can. You can be your own hero. Write your own success story. Practice tumbling, sinking, rising. You'll land safely at the end.

> ### *It's not easy being a mother.*
> ### *If it were, fathers would do it.*
>
> ~ Dorothy, *The Golden Girls*

K **:** The day I moved into single-parenting, I was weighted with more than cardboard boxes. *Whose pain do I deal with first?* I wondered. *Sometimes Melanie is like an enemy in my own camp.* Once I thought, *I've lost her.*

Her history and past family traditions had crumbled. Nothing stayed the same. For example, birthdays and holidays were negotiated. "I feel like I have to choose," she said. Like that first Mother's Day she dined in a fancy restaurant with Daddy and his girlfriend. "She's so pretty," I was told when Melanie returned. "She'd make a better mother than you." (Was I glad I was treating myself to monthly counseling sessions!)

As a mother I was taking such a beating I needed my cup filled back up. Twice yearly, my mother visited, scenting our kitchen with roasting turkey and creamy noodles. My father repaired the roof. Melanie and I felt cozy and cared for. But I knew I needed someone to talk to other times when Melanie would say, "At Daddy's place I don't have to clean my room or dig dandelions. And we always stop for pizza." It seemed as if Ed was always trying to throw me off balance. He also used information from her to rearrange my plans on the weekends

Melanie was supposed to be with him. Thank goodness my friend Regina taught me to be proactive. "Always have Plan B and C," she said. That meant a baby-sitter on call when a week-end visitation was cancelled and I had my own activities arranged.

Mary, my second mom, telephoned weekly, "What's going on?" she'd ask. I filled her ears with Melanie's visitation tales, such as "trolling for women" with her dad. I ranted, *How dare he?*

One Friday night, friends had to scrape me off the ceiling with a spatula. "I want to come home, Mom. Can you pick me up?" Twelve-year-old Melanie was calling from a bar while she was with her dad for the weekend. The parenting rules I had relied on no longer worked. My days seemed to race further out of control.

Then there were those with this advice: "Put her in a foster home." "Give Melanie to her dad." And "No man will ever want to marry you with your daughter around." Regardless of these comments, I couldn't think of walking away.

Several months later my resolve was confirmed. I ran into a business acquaintance I once worked with. "If your daughter makes it," he said, "it will be with you. You're the best parent for the job."

I committed for the long haul, living what I believe and refusing to play the popularity game. "I can't compete with 'Popcorn Daddy' by giving you everything you want," I once told my daughter. "All I can give you is what I think you need: a love that knows how to say, 'no'; the stability of a home you can call your own; consistency, whether you think I'm old-fash-ioned or a meany; and values like taking responsibility and believing that being a good person is more important than feel-ing good."

We experience moments absolutely free from worry.
These brief respites are called panic.

~ Cullen Hightower

Peanut Brittle Moments

Children of divorce face a terrifying task—understanding why the parents who love, protect, and care for them are causing them distress, fear, confusion, and anger. Children are a reminder that you and their dad once had a history together, like a solid block of peanut brittle now broken into jagged bits. Whose shattering do you handle first? Theirs or yours?

"When a marriage breaks down, most men and women experience a diminished capacity to parent," writes Judith Wallerstein in *Second Chances*, a book about who wins, who loses, and why. "They give less time, provide less discipline, and are less sensitive to their children, being caught up themselves in the personal maelstrom of divorce and its aftermath. Many parents are temporarily unable to separate their children's needs from their own."[3]

According to Wallerstein, a psychologist with over twenty years of research behind her, "The single most important protective factor in a child's psychological development and well-being over the years is the mother's mental health and the quality of her parenting."[4] (Go ahead, scream!)

With another psychologist, Joan B. Kelly, Wallerstein discovered adolescents in psychological difficulty at the time of divorce lacked the inner integration necessary to face complex demands. Others increased in maturity and independence through greater responsibility, not only for themselves, but temporarily for their troubled parents.[5] The authors stress the central hazard for the child is not his own unhappiness, but that family disruption may discourage or interfere with his developmental progress, or move him into a phase for which he is not ready.

"You never get over it; you just get on with it," the saying goes. This is never so true as with children of divorce. Too much is dumped in their laps at one time. They have no context for dealing with the load. They don't know what to do with their emotions or how to cope with potential changes that for them mean big losses. Some children get stuck emotionally at the age they experienced paternal abandonment.

The stakes of parenting are higher now. The children need affirmation and reassurance. They want both parents at home and are coping with their frustration in individual ways. If you have more than one child, the dilemma is doubled or quadrupled. One wants to be good but can't help being bad. Another tries to provoke you, all the time hoping to be accepted and approved. A third appears cool but burns with resentment. A fourth lets out all his hostility, then curls up and cries himself to sleep.

Never be embarrassed by your sweaty palms during this unsteady ride. As you try your hardest in what looks like a heart-breaking situation, heed the best-parent rule: Surround yourself with people who reinforce your values, embrace your person-hood, and encourage you to be the best you can be. It may be a friend, family member, or someone you pay seventy dollars an hour to listen to you.

What looks like the worst may be a sign that better is yet to come. Forget about tickets for smoother, slower rides. Hold on to your seat for the duration. Your children count on it.

Ten Commitments for Single Moms

- I will not go it alone; I will stay in touch with other people.
- I will respect my child for who he or she is.
- I will say "yes" more often than I say "no" and not sweat the small stuff.
- I will discipline in response to what my child does, not who my child is.
- I will define what works and what doesn't.
- I will make time with my child a top priority.
- I will care for myself.
- I will develop a sense of humor.
- I will love my child and show it every day.
- I will walk my talk.

> *I can't go on like this.*
> *(But until circumstances change, I probably will.)*
>
> ∼ Author Unknown

N: "I realize this is not a bad way to live," said my middle daughter, "just different." She had relished the times Dan was there to tuck her in at night. He had placed the first paintbrush into her slender, artistic fingers. She found security in his presence. When I became the custodial parent, Dan saw the girls occasionally and eventually moved away. She was fourteen when he left and, of the three, appeared least able to adjust, in spite of the gentle wisdom she expressed so well at times.

Although we had blowouts, I learned from her that my children are listening. They tune in to each word I say and everything I don't. They notice changing voice inflections and watch body language. They pick up subtle and direct slips of the tongue.

From the beginning, they'd tell me, "Mom, don't! I don't need to know that. He's still my dad, and I'm gonna love him anyway." I turned my experience with divorce into writing for other hurting women—not them—and got better at respecting their need to honor their father. But I drew up short when it came to The Neighbor.

Until the divorce, my children had never heard me swear or utter obscenities. "Girls, there are times when obscenity is appropriate," I told them now. Here in the reality of my hurt, they saw the raw, gritty side of me. Perhaps the fact I didn't cover it up validated their own feelings that divorce is crazy.

One of my friends laughed and helped me not take my new self so seriously. Others quipped, "You're only hurting yourself." Looking back, I think if I had acted differently I would have been lying to myself and to my daughters. I wanted to communicate a sense of moral discernment in a world that puts a spin on the Word of God, saying "Judge not," when an ethical or moral dilemma is presented. Maybe I didn't do it in the best way, but I modeled real-

I GIVE MY CHILD
UP TO GOD

I wrote this letter to the Lord, but in my mind I envisioned holding my daughter up in the palms of my hands and giving her to my ex. He's won! I thought then. Now, I believe my relinquishment of her to the Lord freed Him to work in her life. This letter helped me move on to care for myself and get better so I could take better care of her.

Write a similar one when you are feeling your relationship with a child is out of control or going poorly. As you write, envision yourself holding him or her up in your hands and giving him or her back to God.

ity: that faithfulness is fundamental; what my husband did was outrageous; that deception and betrayal destroy something precious inside a woman; seduction ruins many lives. I pray it will never happen to them, and more importantly, that they will never be a party to anybody else's divorce.

I always wondered how an acquaintance of mine maintained emotional and spiritual equilibrium throughout her ordeal. I struggled with her banal sweetness until I discovered it was not as it appeared. She was dying inside.

Instead of wilting, I reacted because I want to live. When the Space Mountain ride was over, I knew I didn't want to be a "ghost woman." I wanted to seize the lows and savor the highs—and not be scared of the ups and downs of the wildest ride. "Let's do it again!" the girls and I shouted that sunny California day.

Guess what: This year we just might head for Six Flags Magic Mountain, where Superman: The Escape just opened. From zero to 100 mph in seven seconds! I wonder if its free fall—the world's fastest—can top my last two years!

> *Children are a great deal more apt to follow your lead than the way you point.*
>
> ∾ Anonymous

Lemonade-Stand Love

"If you are feeling sad [or mad] and tell a child that 'everything is fine,' you are giving a double message," says Isolina Ricci, author of *Mom's House, Dad's House.*[6] She claims demystification of events is very important. "Better to admit, 'I'm sad [or mad] right now,' and then reassure the child, 'But it's not about you and me. It's about grownup matters.'" Ricci believes it is easier for children to deal with the truth than confront whispered hostility, martyred silences, or actions that contradict words.

You know everything is not fine. Divorce and child-custody laws are in a state of flux. The system appears stacked against women and children. Since California passed the first "no-fault" divorce bill in 1969 and forty-nine states followed, the number of divorces in this country surged 68 percent.

"Right now it is legally easier to divorce your spouse of twenty-six years than it is to fire someone you hired last week," says Randal Helman, a former judge and executive of the Michigan Family Forum, a group that lobbies for divorce-law reform.[7]

Under no-fault law, one partner's desire to end the marriage supersedes the other's desire to keep it intact. The balance of power favors the divorce seeker, even if that person has been having an affair and/or abandoned his or her family. Some lawyers say women have lost the opportunity to negotiate more favorable financial settlements. In contrast, others

Dear God,

Tonight I commit to You my daughter. I'm afraid of what's happening. I see her more out of control. What should I do, Lord? You've brought me through hell on earth, anguish unbelievable, and now I have a new problem. This is so hard to deal with—a daughter I dearly love but do not like and who does not like me or want to be with me.

Tonight I turn this problem over to you, Lord. I ask You to tell me what to do. Help me. I have no one to turn to. You know my health is at risk over this tension. Provide your direction, please. I allow You to work. Help me let go and trust You and wait patiently for You to work.

My life feels on hold until this question is resolved. I start a job with a new agency tomorrow. So many changes in my life. I place my trembling hand in Yours and look ahead (not back) to Your plan for me. I know You have one. Help me not to miss it.

I feel tired. It's 11:35 P.M. Thank You for Your answers. I love You Lord!

Kari

I CAN DO THIS!

Counselors recommend the following guidelines during the first year after a divorce:

- *Expect anger, and establish a safe zone for venting it.*

- *Be prepared for tough questions. Answer briefly and age-appropriately.*

- *Do as much as you can together: chores, play, naps, creative projects.*

- *Make affection a daily habit, even if the children slough it off.*

- *Accept you can't control what they do with your ex-spouse.*

- *Minimize changes in your schedule, neighborhood, church, etc.*

- *Keep your own dating a low priority at first; allow children time to adjust to the idea.*

- *Affirm and reassure the divorce is not their fault.*

claim a system based on fault stacks the deck against the party with less economic power—usually the woman.[8]

All moms are at risk: some lose custody if they are too successful; others if they aren't. Attorney Marcia Clark's ex-husband sued for custody of their two sons because she was "too busy working." As you navigate your own dark labyrinth, you give your children what you can. Some ex-spouses are congenial; others, controlling; a few, conniving. You work with what you get, and you pray for what you need. You leave the unfairness of it all and your inability to right the wrongs with Someone stronger (Prov. 23:10-11). You hold together what's left of family. You compromise with your betrayer to protect and provide for your children.

Getting caught in power struggles with your children about how nice Daddy's condo is or how much he spends entertaining them impedes progress. It wastes precious emotional energy. It's time to convey the most important message to your children: "I care about you." Focus on communicating that you cannot give them what you and they most want: an intact family. Your children will ask questions and express confusion. Just be there. And as you wave good-bye to what will never be again, you are promising never to say "I can't help you," and always to say "I'll do what I can."

How to Make Lemonade Out of a Lemon

- If you tend to get emotional or flustered, avoid face-to-face meetings with your ex.

- Set up phone appointments, at your convenience, so you're not caught off guard. Before the call, list points you want to cover.
- Keep your tone strictly business. Hang up before the conversation gets personal or either of you becomes emotional, angry, or irrational.
- Focus on the children's wishes and welfare.
- Avoid making your ex's problems yours. Do not seek empathy for your own. Refuse to mother him.
- Do not be the go-between for your children and your ex or allow your children to be the go-between for you and their father.

K. My daughter is college-age, studying for a degree. She lives with her step-dad and me, rides horses, takes care of our four spoiled and loyal dogs, and works a part-time job. I'm proud of how far she has come. But our life together is not without residuals.

Now I know: divorce terminates a marriage; but it does not terminate a family. Melanie's father is always present in our lives, in visits with her, occasional letters, phone calls, memories, and even fantasy. He was her idol. No wonder I experienced so much resistance from her in the early years. It took days to return to normal living after she came back from Wednesday-night

EIGHT PROMISES
TO MY KIDS

1. *I will try to be the best parent I can be.*

2. *I will be accountable so you can reach me anytime, and I expect the same courtesy of you.*

3. *I will make time during the week just for you.*

4. *I will not burden you with my problems, allowing you to be a child, not my caretaker.*

5. *I will care for myself by eating healthfully, exercising, maintaining a social life, seeking help when I need it, and spending quiet time with God daily.*

6. *I will try to model the virtues and values I talk about: honesty, hard work, compassion, thrift, fairness, forgiveness, acceptance.*

7. *I will not speak against your other parent; I will apologize when I do.*

8. *I will try to live out this definition of success: getting up one more time than I am knocked down.*

(P.S. When I try and fail, please forgive me. I love you.)

I'LL DO MORE THAN SURVIVE THE HOLIDAYS

Although survival is a worthy goal in itself the first year after a divorce, you'll probably do even better. You can thrive a little more each year as you implement these tips:

- *If an old tradition fits your new life, repeat it. If it doesn't feel right or there is pain when you think of it, replace it.*

- *Do something you've never imagined: rent an RV and take off for the desert, check into a hotel downtown, visit a friend, work at an inner city shelter, host an open house, organize a potluck dinner, go skiing on Christmas day, bundle up for a New Year's walk on the beach.*

- *Make excuses for parties: last day of autumn, your best friend's grandchild, a child's driver's license, tax return filed, death by chocolate.*

- *Adopt a theme for your home on a symbolic anniversary: The Year of Light—string up tiny lights all over your house; The Year of Prosperity—tie bundles of play money on a leafy branch for a centerpiece;*

outings and every other weekend at his place. She was arrogant, authoritarian, and verbally abusive.

"I'm being the best parent I can," I told Melanie. When I no longer had energy to argue over homework, I allowed her to fail high-school algebra the first time through. When she returned from a sixteenth-birthday trip with her dad and said, "I'm going on a blind date Friday, like it or not," I arrived at a turning point. Melanie already knew the parameters around her dating: Mom gets to meet the boy and whoever drives. This time she vehemently objected and said that her dad had joint custody and had given her permission because she needed to be in a serious relationship by the time she was eighteen. Although I could not rush the settling of her undulating emotions, I refused to be held hostage any longer in my own home.

I pulled out her suitcase and said: "Then your dad can have total responsibility raising you. I won't watch you destroy yourself and pick up the pieces afterwards." Her door slammed. I trembled. She stayed.

Now there is little she and I can't talk about. We're learning to fight fair, fast, furious, and in five minutes. Then it's over.

"I make mistakes," I still tell her. I think she's getting the idea that home and family aren't about a big house and perfect people, but about listening ears. Open hearts. Warm hugs. I think she's catching on that whatever happens, her mom is her biggest fan.

For me, single-parenting coincided with her teenage years. Some of the harrowing adventure would have happened without the divorce. But does a mother ever get over how divorce hurts her child? As Psalm 69:4 says: "Though I have stolen nothing, I still must restore it." By staying through the ride, I hope I'm showing Melanie the way home.

Wrapping Up the Holidays

When you're pacing the floor because holiday weekends are too quiet or you have nowhere to go, remember it's a fallacy that the whole world has a date on New Year's Eve, receives valentines in February, and serves Easter brunch.

What to do when family-packed jeeps and boats pull out of neighborhood driveways on summer holidays? Sit in the sun on your back porch or nap in the shade. And on Thanksgiving or Christmas? Wallpaper over those Currier and Ives images. Curl up on the couch with a great classic video, or chuckle at Chevy Chase in *Christmas Vacation*, thankful all those creatures aren't stirring in your house!

Who takes a child by the hand, takes a mother by the heart.

~ Danish Proverb

The Year of Simplicity—store half your decorations and give your walls a fresh coat of paint.

- *Get input from your children as you create new ways to celebrate their birthdays. Mingle those with familiar traditions.*

- *Keep a journal of holidays, including what worked and what did not. Document people's feelings about holidays, including your own. You'll stimulate better ideas for next year.*

- *Redefine Valentine's Day. What does love mean to you at present? If your heart is still bleeding, express that in poetry or art. Pour out your love on the people you love, then buy yourself flowers and write a message affirming the woman you are today.*

- *Start at least one new tradition and one new recipe for each holiday this year.*

- *Fill your home with music, soft lighting, good smells. Make the atmosphere work, and you won't have to.*

- *Plant a dormant amaryllis bulb, and watch hope sprout.*

N: I don't do birthday parties anymore (or help with math homework). My mothering is no longer based on things like that. My kids no longer do picnics or camping. Our bonding experiences as a family are going to be based on radically different criteria. I cling to the belief that the early years mattered more than I realize, and I constantly ask, "How can I facilitate activities together that my daughters enjoy?"

Meanwhile, I go on watering the lawn, stocking the fridge, attending each of my girls' sports events. Some days I look around and marvel at the fact I'm still here! I'm the one who is getting up in the morning to the sound of their alternative music; building the fires; maintaining their home; paying the bills; quelling emotional brush fires; cheering on the pole vaulter, the volleyball player, and two different basketball teams; waiting up nights; and handing out hugs. All without getting burned out, beat up, or bled dry. Anybody who wants to can criticize me, blame me, accuse me of anything they want. But I'm still here. That fact speaks with more eloquence that anything else I could possibly say. (So I won't.)

The greatest ability is dependability.

〜 Anonymous

On the Right Track

Not one single mom we talked to says the ride is smooth. Maybe you are hitting the big curves right now. You are always defending your actions and reactions. You're not a failure. You are doing the best you can. Nobody else can fill your seat. You keep focused on being the best parent you can be. In the end, that's what counts.

15

I'm Laughing Again

He will yet fill your mouth with laughter
and your lips with shouts of joy.

~ Job 8:21, TLB

She stood in the doorway watching him. He didn't see her until he closed the car door. In the silvery moonlight, slender shadows danced with the slick icy sidewalk. Billy Boy strolled into the house.

"Come on in," said Sandra Sue. "I've been waiting for you." With a toss of her long blond mane, she smiled.

Billy Boy could see in those baby blue eyes and luscious lips that Sandra Sue meant business. "I've come for what's mine," he said.

"I know, Babe," she said, sauntering toward the stairway.

"Take it off," Billy Boy said, pointing to her creamy velour robe. "Half of everything's mine—including your clothes."

"Fine," said Sandra Sue. "No problem." She dropped the robe at his feet and climbed the stairs. "You know where my closet is. Go ahead. See what fits!" Her silhouette disappeared behind the shower door.

Later, Billy Boy drove into the sunset with his bimbo by his side and half the "community" property in the trunk of his BMW. Sandra Sue settled into her favorite cushy chair. She stretched her long lanky legs onto the flower chintz ottoman. As "101 Strings" strummed, she picked up her dog-eared copy of *When He Leaves*. The pages fell open and in the flickering firelight, she read: *There is a time for everything.*

"You've got that right," Sandra Sue laughed. "Tomorrow it's time to go shopping!"

233

If you've gotten to this chapter,
you know the joke's on him!

    ~ Kari

Lightening Up the Easy Way

Your luster is lasting. And so is your smile. But it's more than a sunny disposition. There's light behind your eyes and passion in your voice. You're laughing again.

You are not a dry-clean-only item. Stiff. Starched. Confined inside a stuffy bag. You're one swanky number who is comfortable with yourself. You've been through life's hot water and come out knowing what's true about yourself. You're not embarrassed by a little wear and tear or wrinkles. You are no longer hanging out in the back of the closet.

What matters now isn't the way you looked to him or what he took from you but the adventure of every tomorrow. "He turned my sorrow into joy!" wrote the psalmist. "He took away my clothes of mourning and gave me gay and festive garments" (Ps. 30:11-12, TLB). It's time to go shopping with God.

Today's women don't have hot flashes.
They have power surges.

    ~ New Saying

Get the Last Laugh

"Happy hormones" like immunoglobulin and cytokines, experts say, fight bacteria and viruses and destroy tumors. Just a quarter hour of belly laughing is enough aerobic activity to stimulate and increase the level of these hormones. Laughter stimulates blood circulation and oxygenation that promotes clear thinking. It increases "natural killer" white blood cells, according to researchers Lee Berk and Arthur Stone.[1] Their studies suggest healing is accelerated in people who laugh.

"Put on a happy face" and "Fake it till you make it" are good advice. Other research shows that even the act of smiling when you don't feel like it can reduce stress and improve your mood. Not only does it elicit positive responses from others, but it promotes a sense of well-being. According to psychologist Paul Ekman of the Human Interaction Lab at the University of California in San Francisco, real smiles and fake smiles produce identical changes in brain activity, skin temperature, heart rate, and respiration.[2]

"You can't just sit around waiting for the inspiration to become happier to strike you," says Dr. David Myers, professor of psychology at Hope College in Holland Michigan, citing an international study of 170,000 people. "But it can help you take steps in the right direction." Myers believes after researching hundreds of scientific studies on happiness, that with practice attitudes can follow behavior.[3]

Nobody ever died of laughter.

∽ Max Beerbohm

Let Life's Absurdities Tickle You Pink

Do whatever it takes to release those happy brain chemicals. Start exercising that muscle attached to your funny bone. With practice, you'll get the hang of it. Begin by compiling a humor profile. What were your favorite pass-the-time moments as a child? What activities made you really happy? Was it slapping together mud pies in the sandbox? playing "Skip to My Lou"? fishing with your big brother? flying kites? What did you beg your mom and dad to do over and over again? As you grew up, what Sunday funnies did you read and which comedians made you crack up? These are keys to what make you feel good now.

> *Comedy is tragedy—plus time.*
>
> ~ Carol Burnett

Make a laughter scrapbook. Fill it with cartoons, jokes, stories, funny greeting cards, kids' sayings, and overheard comments that make you laugh. Read the funnies faithfully. Ask people to save and send you things that are humorous. Keep a pencil and paper by the TV so you can record one-liners that get you giggling. Spend a half hour chuckling at the card store. Write anything funny in your notebook.

> *Few women admit their age. Few men act theirs.*
>
> ~ Author Unknown

Build a play box. Collect small toys, gag gifts, and whimsical items that are fun, colorful, and cuddly. Take a chuckle break and delve into it. Pull out a bottle of bubbles and blow them around the office. Disguise your voice with a foreign accent, and leave a mysterious message on a friend's answering machine. Call your sister, and tell her the latest "knock" joke. Ask your kids for crazy riddles and rhymes.

> *You can tell it's going to be a bad day when:*
> - *You put your bra on backwards and it fits better.*
> - *You call suicide prevention and they put you on hold.*
> - *Your blind date turns out to be your ex-husband.*
>
> ~ Passed on at the Pithy Pity Party

Cultivate wacky humor in your family. Sometimes you have to turn to outside sources and a context totally beyond your own environment. When you find something everybody laughs at, you know it's a treasure. If you're tuned in, you can even turn insults into hilarity. Twist slaps into compliments; you'll drive your enemies crazy.

> *Climb every mountain!*
> *Ford every stream!*
> *Follow every rainbow!*
> *(That oughtta reduce middle-age spread.)*
>
> ∾ Author Unknown

Ask: What will be important 100 years from now? That you got mad at your teenager's latest insult and tried to set him straight, or that you turned it into an occasion to laugh? You might also lift his heavy burdens, not by trying to "talk" about it, but by leaving things in his room that make him laugh. Tape clever sayings inside closets or tuck them under pillows. Leave a dollar—or five—where someone will find it—in the pocket of favorite jeans, the toe of a shoe or a textbook. Catch him laughing with friends, and take notes on what works. Spread those feel-good hormones however and wherever you can.

> *Laughter is a tranquilizer with no side effects.*
>
> ∾ Arnold Glasow

Loosen Up: Go Ahead and Lose It

It's never too late to loosen up. You are never too old. Celebrate what you thought was impossible by grinning at reality. A 100-year-old woman believed she was way beyond menopause and forever barren. In the end, God handed her a late, great bundle of joy. She laughed and said, "All who hear will laugh with me" (Gen. 21:6).

Even your grandmother used to say, "Laugh and the world laughs with you. Cry and you cry alone."[4] How true that is! Rare friends will be there for you when you express vulnerabilities and need to let the tears flow. But most people don't have broad enough shoulders. They are personally threatened by your loss and don't know what to say about your grief. If you don't pick yourself up, eventually you will lose friends; it's just a fact of life.

Happiness attracts like a magnet. You will get others laughing with you. Laugher sweeps cobwebs out of closet corners and keeps the moths out. Starve the negative, and feed the positive. Make a list of all the good things about being single:

You no longer have to:

- explain buying another pair of shoes to go with the ~~fifteen~~ *Sixteen* you have

- listen to snoring in the middle of the night

- share closet space

- filter things through his schedule

- ask his opinion

- shoo the cat off his car

- wrestle for the remote control

- make notes to remind him of everything

- be late because he won't ask directions

- worry about an unbalanced checkbook

On the weekends he has the kids, you get to:

- sit in the big comfortable chair anytime at all

- turn up the heat as high as you like

- devour every truffle-filled chocolate in the box

- pick out the piece of chicken you really want

- leave dishes in the sink for two days
- turn off *Rocky* reruns
- buy Betty Boop checks
- eat garlic bread
- create order (finally) in the garage

Laugher is a shock absorber
that eases the blows of life.

∼ Author Unknown

Only Your Hairdresser Knows For Sure

N: Sue, my hairdresser, and I sat in her car outside the post office in pouring rain. I'll never forget how embarrassed and humiliated I felt. But I needed her advice on talking to my daughter Christy about Dan's imminent departure. Her son was Christy's long-time boyfriend, and I thought maybe he could help.

"I have something to tell you," I started. She could see I was in shock and said, "Christy is pregnant!" The complete absurdity of her comment took me by surprise. I burst out laughing.

"No," I said. "Dan is having an affair…"

Sue begged me to tell her who the other woman was. I refused.

"Okay," she said, "I'm going to say one name and if that isn't who it is, I'll shut up."

To my complete amazement, she knew.

"Look," Sue said, "I've been in the beauty shop for seventeen years. . . ."

I couldn't help but chuckle. As if it were no big thing, Sue helped me see everything differently. "Tell Dan to move in with her," she advised. "I guarantee he'll be out in fourteen days!"

With a wise, earthy detachment, Sue exposed humor inherent

in my pain. I craved her wit, her ability to make me feel better—unlike my super-spiritual friends who sometimes made me feel worse. That day what I needed most was a good-hearted poke in the ribs.

When Dan eventually approached Sue with his version of our saga, she wasn't fooled. She simply told him, "Noelle did what she had to do to cope with what you put her though."

To all the beauty-shop people everywhere who help us through those bad-hair days, I say, "Thank you for being real. Hurray for hairdressers!"

Angels can fly because they take themselves lightly.

∼ C. K. Chesterton

K **:** Behind every dumped wife is a hairdresser story. For thirty years I've followed my hairdresser, Karen, from shop to shop through life's tragedies to its triumphs. She knew about Ed's affairs before I did. She cut The Neighbor's hair!

"Knowing that I knew and that you didn't know, and not being able to say that I knew, was awful," she says now. Like a rock dropped into a pond, the rippling effect of the affair tested our friendship.

Determined that Ed's actions would not destroy it, I returned each month for a trim. Karen showed me The Neighbor wasn't a vixen but one of many victims. Karen is great at what she does. Who else but a hairdresser could have helped me wash that man out of my hair? By getting to the root of the problem and adding a little color to it, I saw that when Ed got kinky, the "perm" fell out of our marriage.

Today, Karen and I giggle like two school girls about all the players in this comedy of errors: Ed, still acting out the same ol' role; The Neighbor and I, who took our bow years ago and moved on.

Reality is for people who lack imagination!

~ Bumper Sticker

Live on the Wild Side: Go for the Wacky

Hang out with hyenas. Go looking for things that make you crack up and double over. Curl up the corners of your mouth when you meet another person on the street. Keep a joke ready on your lips. Get as wacky as you need to be. Martin Luther said, "If you aren't allowed to laugh in heaven, I don't want to go there." More than a temporary "ha," grins and guffaws imprint joy in your brain and nervous system.

Wasn't it Albert Einstein who said "Imagination is everything"? Why be normal? Open up your soul. You have made it this far. Don't get run down; wind up your wit. Get electric by plugging into humor.

Put on the new [wo]man.

~ Ephesians 4:24

"Queen of Dorkdom." That's what my youngest daughter calls me!

"And proud of it!" I reply.

One man I dated often told me, "You're nutty!" It was the greatest compliment. Had I *ever* before dared to be nutty, a dork, anything other than perfectly sensible?

After a visit with Christy at college one weekend, I asked her to walk me to my car to say good-bye. On the way to the dorm elevator we got to giggling about the rude sound my shoes made on the carpet. Suddenly, the elevator door parted and sixteen people stood staring straightfaced at Christy and me. We regained decorum, got on, and then promptly lost it, giggling all the way down to the ground floor.

THROW A PITHY
PITY PARTY!
*by Michele "I-See-My-Dog-
More-Than-I-See-My-
Husband" Tennesen*

*Feeling the weight of the
world on your shoulders?
Don't be so glum, chum!
Come to a pithy pity party
for the dumped, downsized,
exploited, allergic, neglected,
ignored, bored, and door-
mats. It's the perfect escape
for those who have drops
that spot, no life, bad-hair
days, the heartbreak of
psoriasis, rebellious children,
cranky creditors, and pets
that aren't housebroken.*

*Dress is casual, but wear
sack cloth and ashes if you
prefer.*

*Comfort food snacks, beer
to cry in, and a new deck of
cards (so you can change
the hand life's dealt you)
will be provided.*

*Please join me for this
chance to laugh at life and
ourselves!*

> *Learn to laugh at your troubles
> and you'll never run out of things
> to laugh at.*
>
> ∼ Lyn Karol

K. "Wipe that smile off your face," my parents often told my brother and me. "Don't laugh at the table or you'll be crying afterwards." I took their advice the way they meant it: seriously. My great-grand-parents homesteaded the prairie in dugouts, and their stern midwestern life-is-tough mentality was passed down to me. I inher-ited more somber bones than silly ones.

My adult world was solemn, too; there are few laughs where I worked. So when Ed decided our marriage vows were a joke, I decided to make some changes of my own. I learned to "chill" as my daughter puts it. When she left for high school wearing a pair of those ready-to-drop-off baggy pants, either I had to laugh at myself or check into a psycho ward. Now you should hear us howl in the dressing rooms at Marshalls or Ross. These days Melanie is the one in a tiz over my shopping coups. She won't let me be seen in public with pant legs cut for a flood.

Shopping with Noelle, I talked her into buying the three-inch heels (instead of the two-inch) and a silk shirt that flaps softly open at the neckline. We laughed all after-noon, exchanging parts of our stories we'd never dared tell. The first time I told her, "Someday you'll laugh," she was incredulous.

Our chuckles now are not a spiteful, "ha, ha ha," but an exhale and exclamation: "Aha! Now I get it!"

*The most wasted of all our days
are those in which we have not laughed.*

~ Sebastien Chamfort

She Smiles at the Future...

In the beginning, life was simple. All you wanted was love. A little happiness. Health. A decent haircut. Into your mental scrapbook you pasted snapshots of the man and the marriage that was to last a lifetime. Somewhere along the way, he decided it was not to be.

Now, if you are courageous enough to feel, wise enough to forgive, strong enough to let go, and brave enough to have a vision, you, too, will laugh again.

When he leaves, you decide what will be. Go ahead. Let 'er rip. You know that the joke's on him!

*To laugh often and much ...
that is to have succeeded.*

~ Ralph Waldo Emerson

16

I Am Safe, Secure, And Loved

My people can safely camp in the wildest places ...
I will make my people and their homes
around my hill a blessing....
No one shall make them afraid.

〜 Ezekiel 34:25-26, 28, TLB

K: Bird nests decorate the branches of a ficus tree in my living room. I've been picking them up around my country garden for years. An oriole's palm-threaded hammock. The adobe flat of a swallow. A redwing blackbird's grass hut. A hummingbird suite. The twig-cabin of a scrub jay. And an anonymous shelter created from vacuum fuzz, dog hair, and scraps of twine.

My favorite nest is fashioned from the needles of a Christmas tree we tossed over the hillside a few years back. All summer the sun sizzled. Then winter winds blew. From the sharp, brittle needles of this abandoned Noble Fir, a bird wove a nest that spring. I discovered the masterpiece during fall cleanup. I'm fascinated how the dark needles are laced together with those sun-bleached a dusty grey.

As I clean today, I remove the intricate little nest from its place and cradle it in my palm. At the top is a small opening. Prickly needles were curved around to protect the brood once nestled inside the tightly woven basket.

The nest affirms and inspires me. I know something about this: How the prickly protects. Finding something useful in discarded stuff that had lost meaning for someone else. Weaving past with present to cradle the future. The care and feeding of fledglings: my daughter and my incubating dreams. Not long ago I felt like that tossed-out Christmas tree. Discarded in midlife. Over the hill. Left alone to make it or break it.

247

One season followed the next. So much more has come. My life was created, not by accident but by design. I am discovering beauty in change. Making peace with contrast. Accepting uncertainty. Learning to like it here.

A man who strays from home
is like a bird that wanders from its nest.

∼ Proverbs 27:8, TLB

Spring Is a Time of Incubation

No matter what season the calendar says, in your life it is spring; time for a new beginning. This season you and God are forming a weather-tight fortress made from whatever is available and profitable. This crash pad will house and protect your brood, your spirit, and your soul from predators and the elements until you are ready to fly. You are nesting, resting within the rustic comfort of this place. Some memories still prick when you go in and out and about your work. But you are safe here and secure. And never forget—you are loved.

He keeps his eye upon you as you come and go.

∼ Psalm 121:8, TLB

You Are Safe

You are safe because now you are responsible for yourself. You are no longer living under the influence of an unloving mate. Why he left isn't as important now as living in a way that is consistent with your character and what you know is true. You are safe because you have kept your dignity, your reputation, and your spirit. Through it all, you have not allowed evil to destroy your soul or take away your desire to live.

To you, home furnishes more than a covering called a house. It feeds inner peace and fosters calmer thoughts. When you pass through the opening of your own nesting place and close the door, you are safe to chat on the phone with your best friend, tuck your children into bed, and to read-till-you-drop words that bring sweet sleep. You may feel lonely when you lie there, but you are not alone. You are praying for angels to guard the four corners of your rooftop. You are putting weariness to rest under the shadow of God's wings.

You are safe when you rely on the people who love you and the power of God. You no longer apologize for the intelligence or personality with which you are endowed, nor the discernment and resilience you've shown. You are protected by the boundaries you have clearly drawn between yourself and toxic people. You are safe because the past cannot control you. Without anger and rage attaching you to him, its power is broken. His unhappiness is his problem; you cannot fix life for him. Your bold commitment to move forward with your life and not fall back into old patterns is a barrier that he cannot penetrate.

You are breaking free of thoughts that harm your health and the worry that cuts off faith, strangles peace, and kills joy. You have stopped being your own worst enemy. Because you deserve God's best, you won't settle for less than that. You are covering blank walls with pictures of where you'd like to be. Portraits of hope. For the rest of your life, you will look for pivotal moments sandwiched between ordinary days.

> *Some people are always grumbling*
> *because roses have thorns.*
> *I am thankful that thorns have roses.*
>
> ~ Alphonse Karr

N: A friend came over the other day to ask one of my daughters to baby-sit. We got to talking about other things, and she confided that although she reconciled with her husband after his affair, she still feels a hole in her heart. "My love for him is not innocent and sweet the way it used to be," she said.

Sadness filled me. Seeing them back together playing with their kids or working in their yard while I tackled mine alone, I'd always felt a little envious, thinking, *That's the way it is suppose to happen.* Hearing her confession pulls me back to reality. No longer does my friend feel 100 percent safe in her husband's presence. I wanted to run over and shake that man. "Love her, you fool," I wanted to say. "Court her; give her yourself. Don't you understand what your mistake cost her?"

Now I know things will never be the same for either her or me. I don't know which is harder: being divorced and starting all over, or like her, trying to put the pieces back together in the same, yet different, relationship. We have both been through something profound. I have decided to let it add something to my life rather than take away. It has given me an authenticity, an authority that wasn't there before, and a sense of presence with myself.

Am I being realistic? I don't know. But that's the beauty of redesign. You get another chance to tweak and flex as you go along. Nothing has to be perfect the first time—or ever. The more unexpected twists, the more creative you become in weaving it all together. I work hard at this, and I guess it shows. Yesterday I ran into the counselor who helped me through my earliest trauma. "You look good," she kept saying—as if she couldn't quite believe it.

> *One can never consent to creep*
> *when one feels an impulse to soar.*
>
> ～ Helen Keller

You are Secure

You are secure because you have created sanctuary from recycled bits and pieces of your life. You have built it all in the shelter of sturdy, steady branches that bend with the wind. You are no longer vulnerable to the pseudo-provision of another person who did not have your best interests at heart.

The psalmist writes about security that comes from hands and fingers trained for daily battles and all-out war. God stands between you and your concerns and subdues them under you. Because of this, you seize each day even when you are trembling. You know that you can reinvent your life and redesign your nest as you see fit, as the Lord leads, as weather permits. You have spiritual guidelines that have been tested and tried.

Your security is not tangible, like a retirement account, a family inheritance, or life insurance policies. Your security comes from the inside out, from new emotional rules that push you toward your calling. You refuse to spend another day with the guilt that you could have done more. You know that no one can heal another's wounds. And you don't tolerate abuse anymore, just as you don't do gravy. You are learning when to move out of your own way.

No longer are you tied to other people's opinions or shaken by their criticism. Their definitions don't hold you back or pen you in. You are making distinctions that will pull you like a magnet toward God's will. You are incubating dreams. Believe it or not, you're in the right spot at the right time. You are here for a reason. Determine to live it out.

> *Merely sustaining life is a vegetative state....*
> *Thoroughly living life requires initiative,*
> *risk-taking, sustained action against odds,*
> *sacrificing for ideals and for others, leaps of faith.*
> *People who lead such lives report being happy,*
> *hopeful and exhilarated; even when they fail.*
>
> ⁓ Dr. Laura Schlessinger

K. Five years ago, with dreams of apple pie, I carved a hole in the hard clay. I pounded a stake and tied a five-gallon tree to it with a strip of insulated wire. Over time, the trunk continued to grow over and around the restrictive wire. Today all that's visible is an inch scar ringing the trunk. I can't push the wire in or pull it out, but the tree has learned to live with it.

I am growing around and over life's "if onlys" just the way my tree did. Etched in my mind is not only the painful experience of divorce but God's faithfulness. I learned how important it is to press on with hope even when circumstances and changes would hold me back. To live with my scar, I've had to accept it as one of life's contrasts. Divorce is one piece in the collection of fragments that make up the whole of my life.

I understand when a friend says, "I can't do this anymore." I hear myself saying the same words in an office conference room years ago. After downing three cups of stale coffee, I wondered if I could hold back tears long enough to do my job that afternoon. But I did.

Somehow, one season at a time, I grew over and around my hampering wire. There's a certain security in the ongoing process of living. I can't live a year in a moment. I can't plant a fruit tree today and eat pie tomorrow. Each day I hope my life paints a word picture of what Anne Frank wrote: "I don't think of all the misery, but of all the beauty that still remains."[1]

And we know that all things work together for good
to those who love God,
to those who are the called according to His purpose.

∽ Romans 8:28

You Are Loved

You are loved whenever you enhance the life of someone else. You are loved when you choose to embrace your own life. When you act in loving ways toward yourself, you affirm what your heavenly Father says about you.

You are loved when you decide to accept and try to understand others regardless of who they are or how they treat you. You are loved when you welcome into your life the relentless lover, Almighty God. You are loved when you nurture intimacy with your family, passion for daily adventure, and devotion to the kingdom of heaven.

When you surround yourself with grand books, great music, and good people, you are loved. You are loved when you take care of both body and soul. You are loved when you reach out to touch the world: children, babies, the elderly, animals, the velvet petals of a blossom, and raindrops. Love comes when you hug others and allow them to come close enough to hug you. When you laugh or surprise yourself. When you follow your convictions, do what you know is right, live with a clear conscience. When you follow the way of the pure-hearted. When you hold tightly to the truth.

You are God's dearly beloved and the object of His affection. Chosen. The apple of His eye. Heir to His kingdom. He planned the redemption He makes real in you every day. When you respond by living your life with meaning, you reveal your commitment to the covenant between you and Him. You owe it to yourself and to God to remember all the experiences of life, even if you feel they were unhappy. Living is about reconciling yourself to contrasts, like sweet and sour, as well as every nuance in between. Accepting you are loved by God in spite of crises is a life-changing decision.

Love is a celebration of thanksgiving for receiving all you need to live fully. You fall out of love when you get hung up on what you want—the perfect husband, perfect marriage, perfect kids. A charmed life. You fall out of love when what you thought you deserve gets in the way of gratitude for what you already have and always had.

You are loved because you take responsibility for your shortcomings, changing what you can and letting the Lord work on the rest (Ps. 138:8). You are loved because you belong in this world. To bless and not curse—or cure. To worship by using your gifts and talents to cultivate beauty and replenish hope. To care enough to make a difference. To love. In heaven's eyes, you are not half of something broken, you have been made whole.

His banner over me was love.

∿ Song of Solomon 2:4

N: My nest will soon be empty. My twenty year old, in college, working, and (almost) engaged, has already left the nest. My seventeen year old is taking test flights and flits home at intervals daily. I hear the wings of my thirteen year old fluttering, and I wonder, "Where will I put my passions and energy? Where do I fit?"

I feel God saying, "Get your house in order." I'm on the brink of something new. But what do I do first?

"The next thing," says author Elisabeth Elliot.

I am incubating my fragile dreams. I cradle the thought that one day their shells will crack. With careful feeding, something in my life will take flight.

Love makes you present in your own life.

∿ Whitney Otto

A Time for Flight

The most beautiful and useful things in your life are those characterized by simplicity. You are off the hillside and in the process of redesign. The real love affair begins now. God is working with you. You are working with yourself.

You are coming to terms with your aloneness. It has nothing to do with whether you are in a new relationship or remarried. Being a couple is not validation for who you are. You are your own best companion. You are whole. When you are lonely, you accept that emotion as a universal cry of humanity. You are created for God and community. When you hurt, you migrate to people who know what to say to help you heal. You call them up. You seek them out. And you see that their wise counsel cost them dearly. Like you, their lives are woven with the contrasts of adversity and resilience. They offer credible comfort.

You count on others to be there. But even if they are not, you begin to believe in yourself. And you believe the almighty God loves you through each changing season. You can bet your life on the fact that He is a lover who will never leave.

Faith goes up the stairs that love has made
and looks out the window which hope has opened.

∼ C.H. Spurgeon

～ Epilogue

*A*s we write the last few lines, dot the *i*'s and correct misplaced commas, wrapping up the final manuscript, our lives are still unfolding ...

N: I finally had skylights installed, those symbols of clarity I prayed and planned for more than two years ago but had to postpone when Dan left. The change they make in my northeast living room is greater than I had imagined, like the changes in my life since becoming single again. It would seem the story's come full circle in a way, clear and calm, but the story's never over. This week, The Neighbor moved back, too, just around the corner.

I've decided to let her presence remind me of how far I've come. I have been given the best part, knowing who I am, and that I am exactly where I'm supposed to be. Sometimes the hurt comes back. But so does the sun, one day at a time. And I intend to revel in its ever-changing light.

K: After communicating with her dad, my daughter slipped into depression, this time requiring hospitalization. A friend, listening to my concern, hurt my feelings when she said, "I don't think you've gotten over your divorce issues."

But I take heart. I know after today's sunset comes tomorrow's sunrise. Enveloped in the days that follow are moments to try again. My dog Amber lies at my feet waiting for a romp outdoors. I can hear Sigmund, the goat, bawling for his daily treat of fresh-cut withered roses, thorns and all. Then there's Richard, wondering if life will ever be back to normal when this book is finished. I wonder if it ever was. We laugh.

～

You are not alone. With us, you are going through something profound. Perhaps you still cannot make sense of it. When godless powers work overtime, it is to divert your progress. They want you stuck in the shadows of your fear and their lies. A consequence of divorce is that the old luggage you thought you had stashed away keeps falling out and flopping open. From time to time you have to resort and repack the same stuff. Don't let that fact rattle you. This is simply the way it is.

Although you cannot once and for all vindicate the truth, you hold tightly to it. You know truth needs no defense. So when you can't go back, you go on. Each step you take forward moves you toward life and light. You will never know how many others will be helped along the way.

We whisper, "Keep moving; keep going."

Your snapshots are still developing.

~

The Power of Divorce Is an Illusion

It doesn't rip off your relationship with God.
It wilts under the heat of passion for life.
It stops short of robbing every hope.
It fades in the light of good humor.
It doesn't disrobe you of dignity.
It cannot take your courage.
It is dis-empowered by joy.
It capitulates to optimism.
It is disarmed by truth.
Its pain is temporary.
It is starved by faith.
Its time is limited.

(You'll see!)

You are DivorceWise when you know:

You can live and let live.
Just because you lost love,
Doesn't mean you won't have the last laugh!

We invite your sage advice, whimsical comments and single-parenting tips. In the future we hope to include them in a book.

Visit Kari West's web site at www.gardenglories.com for more information about and the Divorce Wise Newsletter- available online or by writing P.O. Box 11692, Pleasanton, CA 94588

∾ Endnotes

Reasonable care has been taken to trace ownership of the materials quoted from in this book and to obtain permission to use copyrighted materials, when necessary.

Chapter 2

1 Harold Arnold Walter, Joseph Yates Peek, "I Would Be True."
2 William J. Gaither, "Because He Lives," (1971).

Chapter 3

1 Noel Paul Stookey, "Wedding Song," Public Domain Foundation, Inc., (1971).

Chapter 4

1 Michael Haederle, "Divorcees Say, 'Take This!' To Their Rings," *Los Angeles Times.*
2 Helen Richards, "God's Protection During War and Peace" (broadcast interview), Tape No. CS 332/2131 (Colorado Springs, Colo.: Focus on the Family).
3 "The Sad Truth About Christians and Marriage," *The Barna Report,* Premiere Issue, pp. 5, 6.
4 Karen Peterson, "A smattering of 'secrets' from successful couples," *USA Today,* Feb. 27, 1996; excerpted from Neal Clark Warren, *The Triumphant Marriage: 100 Extremely Successful Couples Reveal Their Secrets* (Colorado Springs, Colo.: Focus on the Family, 1996).
5 Peter Kramer, "For Better or Worse," *Elle,* September 1997, pp. 306-308.
6 Michael Gartner, "Values? What about divorce?" Counterpoints section, *USA Today,* June 6, 1995, p. 13A; excerpted from 1995 edition of *Information Please Almanac.*
7 Karen Peterson, "Divorce needn't leave midlife women adrift." Health and Behavior section, *USA Today,* April 23, 1993, p. 7D.

8 "Divorces carry financial sting for many middle-age women" *The Daily Review,* April 29, 1993, p. A-1, 16; excerpts from U.S. Census Bureau Data 8.

9 Gail Sheehy, *New Passages: Mapping Your Life Across Time* (G. Merrit Corp, 1995).

10 Philip Yancey, *Where Is God When It Hurts?* (Grand Rapids, Mich.: Zondervan, 1990) p. 207.

11 Jim Smoke, *Growing Through Divorce* (Eugene, Ore.: Harvest House, 1995) p. 150.

12 Dwight Small, *Remarriage and God's Renewing Grace* (Grand Rapids, Mich.: Baker Book House, 1986) p. 43, 50, 51 (condensed).

13 "What Crisis?" *Life,* November 1995, p. 76.

Chapter 5

1 C.S. Lewis, *Mere Christianity* (N.Y.: Macmillan, 1952) pp. 173-174.

2 Philip Yancey, *Disappointment with God* (Grand Rapids, Mich.: Zondervan, 1988), p. 204.

3 Richard Foster, "A Prayer for Rage," *Prayers from the Heart* (San Francisco, Calif.: HarperSan Francisco, 1994).

Chapter 6

1 Barbara Lang Stern, "Your Well Being," *Vogue.*

2 *Ibid.*

3 John Townsend, *Hiding from Love* (Colorado Springs, Colo.: NavPress, 1991), p. 62. Townsend's current practice is Cloud-Townsend Communications, 260 Newport Center Drive, Ste. 430, Newport Beach, CA 92660.

4 Brenda Hunter, *Beyond Divorce* (Old Tappan, N.J.: Fleming Revel, 1978) p. 141.

5 *Ibid.*, p. 36.

6 Launa Herrmann, "Beyond the Anger of Divorce," *The Plain Truth,* March/April 1997, p. 20.

7 Archibald Hart, *Growing Up Divorced* (Ann Arbor, Mich.: Servant Publications, 1991) pp. 105, 106.

8 Philip Yancey, *Disappointment with God* (Grand Rapids, Mich.: Zondervan,

1988) p. 94.

9 Michael Ryan, "Go Ahead, Cry," *Parade,* Jan. 5, 1997.

10 M. Scott Peck, *The Road Less Traveled* (N.Y.: Simon & Schuster, 1978) p. 278.

11 John Townsend, *Hiding from Love* (Colorado Springs, Colo.: NavPress, 1991) pp. 100, 101.

12 Marlee Alex, "Family Values," *Aspire,* January 1997, pp. 19, 20.

Chapter 7

1 Eugene Peterson, *The Message* (Colorado Springs, Colo.: NavPress, 1993) p. 353.

2 Elinor Levy, Ph.D., and Tom Monte, "The Medicine Within," *Ladies' Home Journal,* April 1997, p. 58; and Catherine Houck, "When Stress Gets Under Your Skin," *Good Housekeeping,* May 1996, p. 52.

3 Gerald Sittser, *A Grace Disguised* (Grand Rapids, Mich.: Zondervan, 1996).

4 Jan Miller Girando, Mary Engelbreit, illus., *Don't Look Back* (Kansas City, Mo.: Andrews and McMeel, 1994) last page.

Chapter 8

1 Tom Carter, ed., *2200 Quotations from the Writings of Spurgeon* (Grand Rapids, Mich.: Baker Books, 1988) p. 123.

2 Jack Hayford, *A New Time and Place* (Sisters, Ore.: Multnomah, 1997) p. 1.

3 *Ibid.,* p. 25.

4 *Ibid.,* pp. 27, 29.

5 Joni Eareckson Tada, "Seeing the Impossible." *Moody Magazine,* November 1993, p. 32.

Chapter 9

1 James Hillman, *The Soul's Code* (N.Y.: Random House, 1996) pp. 41, 43.

2 Ron Lee Davis, *A Forgiving God in an Unforgiving World* (Eugene, Ore.: Harvest House, 1978) p. 44.

3 C.S. Lewis, source unknown.

4 Ingrid Trobisch, *Keeper of the Springs* (Sisters, Ore.: Multnomah, 1997)

p. 9.

5 "Newseyes: Give up the family jewels," *The Daily Review,* September 28, 1995, p. A-2.

6 Cathy Horyn, "Diana Reborn," *Vanity Fair,* July 1997, p. 71.

7 Joni Eareckson Tada, Joni Appointment Calendar 1986 (World Wide Pictures, 1985) January entry.

Chapter 10

1 Historical data provided by Judy Buckingham, wife of Crater Lake National Park Head Ranger, George Buckingham in a 1997 interview with Kari West.

2 Archibald Hart, *Growing Up Divorced* (Ann Arbor, Mich.: Servant Publications, 1991) p. 105

3 Malcolm Boyd, *Rich with Years* (San Francisco, Calif.: Harper/San Francisco, 1994) entry for Feb. 7.

4 Sally Stich, "When to Forgive Him," *Ladies' Home Journal,* October 1995, p. 94.

Chapter 11

1 Sonya Friedman, "Isn't It Time to Please Yourself?" *Redbook,* February 1991, p. 154.

2 Deirdre Donahue, "A Tragic Peak," *USA Today,* April 24, 1997, pp. D1, D2.

3 Anne Taylor Fleming, "The Other Side of the Mountain," *Ladies' Home Journal,* June 1997, p. 134.

4 Sonya Friedman, p. 154.

5 Dwight Small, *Remarriage and God's Renewing Grace* (Grand Rapids, Mich.: Baker Book House, 1986) p. 167.

6 Panel discussion with Laurie Hall, Noelle Quinn, and Kari West, "The Hidden Enemy of Marriage," Tape No. CT 009/1709 (Colorado Springs, Colo.: Focus on the Family).

7 "The Sad Truth About Christians and Marriage," *The Barna Report,* Premiere Issue, pp. 5, 6.

8 Ray DeVries, *Westmont College Alumni Newsletter,* February 1988, p. 3.

9 *Ibid.*

10 *Ibid.*

11 "Ravages of Divorce," *The Barna Report,* vol. 1, no. 4:6.

12 Monica Gyulai, "Study finds divorce deeply scars kids," *The Daily Review,* June 3, 1997, pp. B-1, B-2.

13 Judith Wallerstein, Sandra Blakeslee, *Second Chances* (N.Y.: Tichnor & Fields, 1989) p. 300.

14 "A Safe Place," *Virtue,* May/June 1994, p. 65.

15 "Your letters," *Virtue,* January/February 1997, p. 8, referencing "Tis the Season for Turmoil" by Kari West, *Virtue,* November/December 1996, pp. 37-40.

16 "Your letters, *Virtue,* March/April 1997, p. 10 (referencing Kari West article).

17 Sam Keen, *The Passionate Life* (N.Y.: HarperCollins, 1992) p. 248.

18 Jerry Bridges, *The Practice of Godliness* (NavPress, Colorado Springs,1983) p. 216.

Chapter 12

1 Dory Hollander, *101 Lies Men Tell Women and Why Women Believe Them* (N.Y.: HarperCollins, 1995) p. 271.

2 "Medinews," *Ladies' Home Journal,* October 1995, p. 104.

3 Nancy Wartik, "The surprising link to longer life," *McCalls,* June 1997, p. 108.

Chapter 13

1 Historical data provided by Alameda County, CA research librarians and "Winchester Mystery House," published for Winchester Mystery House, San Jose, CA.

2 Random House *Webster's College Dictionary* (N.Y.: Random House, Inc, 1996).

3 *Ibid.*

4 John Townsend, Henry Cloud, *Boundaries* (Grand Rapids, Mich.: Zondervan, 1992) p. 105.

5 Patricia Evans, *The Verbally Abusive Relationship* (Holbrook., Mass.: Bob Adams, Inc., 1992) p. 13.

6 Material provided in an interview of Jeff Klippenes by Kari West, Oct.

1997.

7 Reed Karaim, "The Debate Over What the Bible Says," *USA Weekend*, Oct. 3-5 1997, p.10.

8 Townsend, *Boundaries*, p. 109.

9 *Merriam-Webster's Collegiate Dictionary*, Tenth Edition (Springfield, Mass.: Merriam-Webster, Inc., 1995).

10 Marlee Alex, "Enhancing the Larger Life," *Virtue*, Jan./Feb. 1993, p.22.

11 Isabella Rossellini, *Some of Me* (N.Y.: Random House, 1997), quoted in *Ladies Home Journal*, September, 1997.

12 Andrea Stone, "President's daughter makes up for lost time," *USA Today*, May 7, 1997, p. 4D.

Chapter 14

1 Statistics compiled by M. Franco Salvoza from National Fatherhood Initiative, "Father Figures," *USA Today Weekend*, June 14-16, 1996, p. 5.

2 David Proenoe. "Life Without Father," *Readers Digest*, Feb. 1997, p. 65, condensed from *Life Without Father* (N.Y.: Simon & Schuster, Inc., 1996).

3 Judith Wallerstein, *Second Chances: Men, Women & Children a Decade After Divorce* (N.Y.: Tichnor & Fields, 1989) p. 301, 302.

4 Judith Wallerstein, Joan B. Kelly, *Surviving the Breakup* (N.Y.: Basic Books, Inc./Harper Torchbooks, 1980) p. 95.

5 *Ibid*.

6 Isolina Ricci, *Mom's House, Dad's House* (N.Y.: Macmillan, 1980) p. 180.

7 "Tell Us What You Think," *Glamour*, June 1996.

8 *Ibid*.

Chapter 15

1 "Laugh it off and live longer," *The Sunday Times*, Edinburg, Scotland, August 11, 1996, pp: 1, 20.

2 "Mind & Body: World's Cheapest Stressbuster—A Smile," *Good Housekeeping*, January 1995, 27.

3 John B. Thomas, "Health: How to be Happier," *Better Homes and Gardens*, July 1993, pp. 66, 67.

4 Ella Wheeler Wilcox, "Solitude."

Chapter 16

1 Anne Frank, *The Diary of Anne Frank* (N.Y.: Simon & Schuster, 1952), p. 154.

If you liked this book from
ChariotVICTOR Publishing,
check out these great titles. . .

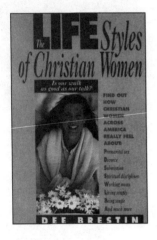

In this book you will meet some of the thousands of Christian women surveyed by Dee. As you learn about these interesting women, you will be challenged to live each day according to God's high calling.

The Lifestyles of Christian Women
by Dee Brestin
ISBN: 0-89693-911-1
Retail: $9.99

This thoughtful book helps us better understand the complexities of friendships and families and their impact on marriage and mothering, taking an honest look at the relationship of sisters, daughters, and the potential volatile relationship between an ex-wife and a new wife.

We Are Sisters
by Dee Brestin
ISBN: 1-56476-604-7
Retail: $8.99

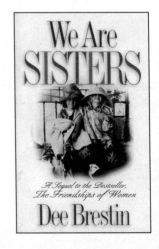

And these great titles. . .

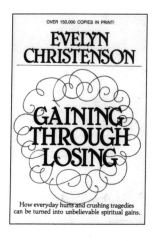

This triumphant book shows how God can take the disappointments and tragedies in life and turn them into unbelievable gains.

Gaining Through Losing
by Evelyn Christenson
ISBN: 0-78143-441-6
Retail: $10.99

Explore the lives of both biblical women and modern-day women who have struggled to find meaning and purpose in life. It is a message of hope for women today, showing that nothing can disqualify them from God's astonishing grace.

If You Only Knew
by Mary Whelchel
ISBN: 1-56476-605-5
Retail: $9.99